HOW TO MAKE MONEY
FROM HOME

HOW TO MAKE
MONEY
—FROM—
HOME

SECOND EDITION

Peter Farrell

KOGAN
PAGE

First published in Great Britain in 1982 by Kogan Page Limited, 120 Pentonville Road, London N1 9JN.
Second edition 1989.

British Library Cataloguing in Publication Data
Farrell, Peter, *1940—*
   How to make money from home: profitable ideas to boost
   your income.—2d ed
   1. Spare-time occupations
   I. Title II. Farrell, Peter,
   1940—. Spare-time income
   331.7'02

   ISBN 0-7494-0039-0
   ISBN 1-85091-905-4—Pbk

Printed and bound in Great Britain by
Biddles Limited, Guildford

Contents

Introduction   **9**

Part I Thinking It Out

1. What's Your Line?   **13**
What do you do? *14*
What do you own? *14*
What are you interested in? *15*
What are you qualified for? *16*
Spare cash? *16*
How much time have you got? *16*
Where do you live? *17*
What kind of person are you? *18*
Do you need a partner? *18*
Selling your product or service *19*
Conclusion *22*

2. Selling Yourself, Your Product or Service   **24**
Basic PR *24*
Selling your product *26*
Getting part-time employment 43

3. You're in Business   **45**
Types of business *46*
Raising money *48*
Employing an accountant *54*
Basic records and bookkeeping *55*
Controlling credit *62*
Annual accounts *68*
Analysing your accounts *75*
Forecasting and cash flow *76*
Costing and estimating *80*

4. You and the Taxman   **85**
Taxable profit *86*
National Insurance *89*
Income tax *90*
Making the most of your tax allowances *92*
Capital Gains and Inheritance Tax *93*

5. **Miscellaneous — But Important**   96
   The law *96*
   Your house *97*
   Insurance *97*
   VAT *98*
   What's in a name? *100*

Part II A Directory of Opportunities

6. **Working for Yourself—a Second Income from
   Your Training, Trade or Profession**   105
   The professions *105*
   Bookkeeping *106*
   Typing *108*
   Consultancy *109*
   Design *111*
   The building trades *112*
   Electrical repairs *114*
   Car maintenance *115*
   Hairdressing *116*
   Teaching *117*

7. **House, Garden and Car**   121
   Taking in lodgers *121*
   Bed and breakfast *123*
   Farm holidays *125*
   Selling garden product *126*
   Jobbing gardening *128*
   Driving a mini-cab *129*
   Running a light removals service *130*

8. **Kids' Stuff**   132
   Babysitting *132*
   Childminding *134*
   Playgroups *136*
   Private tuition *138*
   Organising classes, etc *140*
   Part-time teaching *141*

9. **Cooking and Sewing**   142
   Cooking at home *143*
   Cooking for office dining rooms *145*
   Running a catering service *148*
   Dressmaking *149*
   Knitting *151*
   Ragtrade outwork *151*
   Other sewing work *152*
   Designing and selling clothes *153*

10. **Being Crafty: An Income From Your Craft or Hobby**   155
   Art and design *156*
   Bee-keeping *157*
   Breeding or boarding animals *159*
   Carpentry and cabinet-making *162*
   Making fishing tackle and fly-tying *163*
   China repair *164*
   Metalwork and jewellery *165*
   Model making *166*
   Photography *167*
   Pottery *169*
   Spinning and weaving *169*
   Watch and clock repair *171*
   Toymaking *171*
   Picture framing *172*
   Upholstery *173*
   Saddlery and leatherwork *174*

11. **A Way With Words**   176
   Writing fiction *177*
   Writing non-fiction *181*
   Copy-editing and proofreading *184*
   Indexing *186*
   Translating *187*

12. **Buying and Selling**   189
   Dealing *189*
   Being a mail order agent *191*
   Party plan selling *192*

13. **No Ideas? Jobs Almost Anyone Can Do**   194
   Cleaning *194*
   Being a tea- or dinner-lady *195*
   Distributing leaflets or promotional material *196*
   Market research interviewing *197*
   Waiting *198*
   Being a local councillor *199*

Further Reading from Kogan Page   201

Introduction

The title of this book, *How to Make Money from Home*, might, at first glance, seem like a contradiction in terms; for most of us the home is where we spend the money that we make elsewhere—at the office, in the factory, or out on the road. But however hard we work, we probably still spend more than half our waking hours at home and there is no reason at all why we should not turn some of that leisure time to good account by earning a bit of additional income.

There are also many people, the retired, and those tied down by young children or frustrated by a lack of job opportunities in their area, who have no choice but to stay at home most of the time. For them, earning money from home can not only be a way of helping to meet the household bills but also a means of maintaining a purpose in life and avoiding the boredom and frustration which can so easily set in.

Fortunately, as this book shows, making money from home is now a more realistic proposition than ever before. New technologies, such as the computer and the fax machine, have made communication faster, easier and cheaper; the economic climate favours the enterprising individual who seeks, on however modest a scale, to help him- or herself; the shortage of skilled labour and the disappearance of many small, craft-based industries have left many vacant niches in the market-place which the homeworker can fill; and, for those who want to learn new skills or develop existing ones, the educational and training opportunities are probably richer and more varied than ever before.

Many of us are already earning money, perhaps in a haphazard or desultory way, from our leisure time. This book suggests ways and means in which you can organise those earnings on a regular basis, and ensure that you are maximising your spare-time income and minimising the share of it which goes to the government by way of increased taxes or reduced benefits. If you are going to give up a proportion of your spare time to earning some extra money then it is only prudent to make sure that you are getting as much as possible out of the sacrifice you are making. This means approaching the work in a professional way, making sure that you are not undercharging for your goods or services, finding the best means of selling or publicising them, keeping proper records and not allowing the money you earn to leach away in overhead expenses which you have not costed out thoroughly.

For those who have not yet settled upon a particular line of work, this book aims to give a survey of the vast range of possibilities that exist and to help the reader choose the one that matches his or her talents, circumstances and needs, and the amount of capital and time available.

Working from home can be a source of more than just money; for the retired or the housebound it can be a way of keeping in touch with a wider world; for the handyman or hobbyist it can give a sense of purpose and a yardstick of achievement; and, who knows, it could grow from a spare-time income into a full-time business.

Finally, sexual discrimination has no more place in the home work than in the office of factory. The pronouns 'he', 'him' and 'his' are intended throughout to apply to both men and women and are used only because, in the author's opinion, the circumlocutions of 'non-sexist' language are both clumsy and unnecessary.

Part I
Thinking It Out

1. What's Your Line?

The opportunities for earning money from home are enormously varied, ranging from casual or part-time employment on a temporary basis to the launching of an enterprise which may, with time, grow to be a sole source of income. There are a number of motives for embarking on such a project: it may be that a second source of income is an urgent necessity, or it may be a long-term ambition, perhaps even secondary, in the case of someone who is retired for instance, to a wish to 'keep busy'. An office worker with a long journey at both ends of the day may only be able to work weekends; a mother with children at school may have only the hours between nine and three; a retired person may have all day and every day.

Finding the opportunity that suits you and matches your needs is a process of balancing the 'pros'—the skills, talents, equipment or experience which you can bring to the project—against the 'cons'— the limitations of time, space, money and circumstances which you have to take into account. If you do not already have a very clear idea of the field in which you are going to work, then you will find it helpful to draw up, mentally at least, a balance sheet of the pros and cons which apply in your particular case. In carrying out this process it is important to be realistic, and to remember that a venture undertaken without proper forethought and prudence can turn not into a source of income, but a financial burden and a constant anxiety. But realism must be tempered with optimism and self-confidence; happily there are very few of us who, if we think about it carefully, do not have some 'asset' in the form of knowledge, possessions or experience which can be turned to good account. To help you narrow the field down to those possibilities which are appropriate to your own case, this chapter looks, under fairly general headings, at the considerations you should weigh most carefully.

What do you do?

The most promising starting point in your quest to make money from home may well be your full-time job, especially if you work in one of the professions or have a skilled trade. There are many advantages in doing similar work on your own account to that which you do for your employer: you will know the field, you probably already have many of the necessary contacts and your position as a 'professional' will give both you and your customers confidence. So if you are, say, an architect, a teacher or a motor mechanic, you should weigh up the possibilities of using your professional skills very carefully before passing on to other sources of a spare-time income. The same considerations apply to someone who has retired from such work.

The most obvious drawback to carrying your trade over into your private life may be that when you get home at 5.30 the last thing you want to see is another blueprint, another child, or the underside of another car. You must also consider, of course, whether your employer will be infuriated at the prospect of your setting up in competition with him, on however small a scale; and if your line of work is one which requires expensive equipment or cannot be carried on in the home without driving the neighbours crazy then it is probably best avoided.

Even if your work is such that it cannot be carried out on a spare-time basis—it is hard to envisage a spare-time civil servant or nuclear engineer—you should consider the possibilities of exploiting your knowledge by writing, lecturing, teaching or consultancy work. This can have the added advantage of producing spin-off benefits for your full-time job, by widening your knowledge and experience and increasing your reputation.

What do you own?

After your trade or profession, the next assets you should consider are your possessions. Spare rooms in the house suggest the possibility of taking in lodgers or bed and breakfast guests; a large garden, a greenhouse or just a good outfit of gardening equipment could be the source of an income. Your car will almost certainly be an invaluable addition to any project, or it can be the key to spare-time earnings as a mini-cab.

Even if you are already crowded out of your flat, there is no room to swing a cat in the backyard and you travel everywhere by bus, your catalogue of potentially useful belongings doesn't have to stop there. The tools of your trade, even the equipment accumulated by an enthusiastic do-it-yourselfer, or the gear acquired for a hobby may be useful. Everyday appliances like a sewing machine, a typewriter, or a well-equipped kitchen are also possible bases from which to launch an enterprise.

On the debit side you will, of course, have to consider how far your 'possessions' actually belong to you. If you live in rented accommodation then the lease may well place limitations on its use as a workshop or place of business. Your company may allow you the use of a car for private and family purposes but might well baulk at the thought of it being used as a delivery van.

What are you interested in?

The hobby or pursuit which cannot, in some way, be turned to account as a source of profit has probably not yet been invented. Any leisure pursuit that involves making or repairing things has obvious possibilities; but there are also openings for those who collect, watch, or even just know a great deal about something.

Take the case of bird-watching, a pursuit which, on the face of it, offers few opportunities for making money—until you consider the scores of books and articles about birds, the photographs and illustrations to accompany them, and the increasingly popular bird-watching holidays or cruises. Most of the books and articles are written by amateurs and illustrated by spare-time photographers or artists, and many of the guides on specialist holidays are combining pleasure with the earning of a spare-time income. Whatever your hobby or interest, there are sure to be books written about it, probably a journal devoted to it and very likely people eager to be taught more about it. Someone has to do those things, and if you are nervous about putting yourself forward as an 'expert', remember that most other experts are probably nervous too—the status has as much to do with confidence as with knowledge.

The advantage of turning something that you do for pleasure and interest into a source of income is obvious. Not only will you continue to do something which you enjoy, but because you enjoy it you are likely to do it well. If, for instance, you find sewing and dressmaking a source of fun and satisfaction, but grudge every minute you have to spend in the kitchen, then not only are you more likely to enjoy working as a dressmaker than a cook, but your trouser suits are almost certainly going to be of a much higher quality than your *tripes à la mode*.

What are you qualified for?

It may be that, whatever your present job, you have qualifications or experience in another field. The people most likely to find themselves in this position are probably women who left a job in order to bring up their children and who are now ready to take up a spare-time, if not a full-time, job. But in many other cases as well it can be well worth resurrecting that A level in art or that diploma in education: it could be just the qualification you need to teach in evening classes or to give reassurance at the head of your notepaper.

Spare cash?

Many spare-time occupations will make no call on your savings, but others may require funds to prime the money-making pump. The amounts will vary from under a hundred to several thousand pounds. As discussed in Chapter 3, you can borrow the money you need to start off, but if you do have savings to spare this is certainly a factor you should add to the asset side of your balance sheet of pros and cons, and lack of ready cash or the facility to borrow it will rule out some possibilities. Each entry in Part II gives a rough approximation of the money required to start from scratch.

How much time have you got?

Beyond the relatively simple consideration of how many hours a week or a month you have to spare, there are two other points to bear in mind. First, how urgent is your need of the money? If it is a matter of finding the cash to pay next quarter's gas bill, then you cannot afford to think in terms of a business that will need time to get under way and to build up a clientele. But if you are thinking in the long term, then not only is it possible to lay your plans carefully and start slowly, it may also be feasible to set about acquiring the knowledge or the skill which you will need. Even if, for example, you know all there is to be known about bee-keeping, you cannot hope to pay this year's rates out of your sales of honey if you have not yet bought the hives or the bees; on the other hand, if bees and their habits are a closed book to you but you can afford to wait two or three years, you may have time to start from scratch and learn how to be a bee-keeper.

Second, it is important to reckon up your available time not just in terms of hours per week but also in terms of commitment. If you have always taken a month's holiday abroad in May and intend to continue to do so, then you cannot contemplate, let us say, offering your services as a jobbing gardener; your customers will be very unhappy to see their beds unsown and the weeds flourishing while you cavort on some sunny beach. In the same way, it will be no use trying to start a children's playgroup if you have some other commitment that takes up your time two mornings a week. Again, if you are contemplating making and selling something like speciality foods both you and the shops you supply will be severely handicapped if you cannot ensure regular supplies. This is a particularly important consideration if you are going to offer a service where speed, regularity and promptness are important.

In short, it is essential to work out how far you are able and willing to adapt your routines and your way of life to the demands of your part-time job. In Part II each entry indicates the degree of regular commitment required.

Where do you live?

As has already been mentioned, the place you live in and the space available in it are prime considerations, but another limiting factor may be the susceptibilities of your neighbours. A carpentry business that may be quite tolerable a hundred yards away from the nearest dwelling will quickly bring complaints, and worse, if carried on from a semi on a housing estate.

Moreover, *where* you live as well as the kind of accommodation you live in can be a big factor in what you do or how you do it. A craftsman who lives in a prosperous middle-class district may find plenty of shops in the immediate neighbourhood willing to stock his wares, and customers eager to buy them; but if he lives in an area of high unemployment bereft of craft shops and art galleries, he will find that he must seek either another source of income or an alternative means of selling his products. Similarly, an electrician, who might find more work than he can cope with in an area where many older houses are being done up and restored, could go months without an offer of a job in a new town. Three spare rooms in the centre of a university town may attract a queue of would-be lodgers; ten miles away in the suburbs you may be hard pressed to fill them.

What kind of person are you?

You will stand a much greater chance of gaining profit and pleasure from your spare-time work if you match it to your personality. If, for example, you are someone who finds it intolerable to work alone, then you should avoid a business requiring hours of solitary concentration. On the other hand, if you are never happier than when gossiping to the neighbours and enjoy a vast circle of friends and acquaintances, then you may be ideally qualified to become an agent for a mail order business or to launch into party-plan selling.

If you have always been self-conscious and embarrassed at the prospect of going into a shop and making a simple enquiry, then the chances are that you will not be successful at going into a shop and selling your own products. Any method of earning a spare-time income is going to demand some sacrifice and adaptation on your part, even an effort to steel yourself to do things that you heartily dislike, but it will certainly pay to choose a field that makes use of your strong points and minimises your weak ones.

Do you need a partner?

The advantages of involving someone else in your spare-time enterprise are clear. You share the risk and the work, the weaknesses of one may be the strengths of the other and, most important of all in many cases, you have someone with whom to discuss problems, exchange advice and ideas and to provide moral support at crucial points.

The drawbacks, however, must also be considered. First, far from lessening your risk, a partnership may actually increase it (see Chapter 3). A division of labour can also lead to a division of opinion and interest. If, for instance, one partner undertakes to produce goods which the other is responsible for selling, then a problem can arise that is familiar in much larger-scale industries: the sales side complains that it cannot sell what the production department is equipped for and wants to make and the production department cannot or will not make what the sales side claims it could sell. Instead of a fruitful alliance the partnership becomes a war of attrition.

Relationships which work well when the sun shines can deteriorate when storm clouds loom. A partnership, even a spare-time one, is not to be entered into lightly. In the days of the Raj, one sahib expressed admiration for another by saying that he was 'a good man to go tiger shooting with', meaning that, if things went wrong, he was not the sort of cad who shinned up the nearest tree leaving you face to face with an indignant tiger. Be sure that your partner is not the kind to run for cover when the tigers turn nasty. Nor should he or she be so rash as to try and slay business tigers with a catapult, or so careful that he won't take a step into the jungle without a field artillery battery.

The most obvious partner for many will be a husband or wife, but this is a step to be approached with particular caution. Extending your private partnership into business might bring you even closer together—but it might also drive you further apart. Moreover, involving your husband or wife in a spare-time business could have the effect of depriving you of just the sort of independent advice and counsel you need; looking at your spare-time work as an interested outsider, he or she may be able to see things more clearly, talk to you more easily, and offer help and sympathy more readily than as a part of it.

Selling your product or service

If you have read the first part of this chapter, you should have in your mind a fairly definite idea of what is or is not possible in your particular case, and in the light of this you should assess the suggestions made in Part II. But when you have made your choice from those suggestions, or have come up with a variation on one of them or an original proposition of your own, there is one further, crucial test you must apply: is there a market for what you hope to sell, and if so, can you reach it?

In some cases, of course, this can be determined by simple trial and error. If you have decided that your best bet for making an additional income is to find work as a waiter or waitress, then a look at the 'Situations Vacant' column in your local paper and a visit to half a dozen cafés or restaurants will quickly reveal whether there is any demand for your services.

If you plan to work freelance in your spare time in the same field in which you are employed full-time, then you probably have a pretty good idea of your chances already. Your prospects will be good if the firm you work for has more jobs than it can cope with and is turning customers away; on the other hand, if half of your colleagues have been made redundant and are looking for work you had probably better think again. You may also be in a position to make this kind of judgement if you are thinking of turning your hobby or interest into a source of income. For example, if you know that ten other members of the local camera club are already seeking photographic work, then you will have to take account of some stiff competition.

But in other cases the answer will not be so clear, and you will need to carry out some elementary market research to establish whether there is a demand for your goods or your service.

One obvious place to start your research is in the places you hope to sell your products. If you plan to sell craft objects or food, then some enquiries at local shops will help to determine whether you will be a welcome source of supply or a drag on an overcrowded market. In order to be sure that you are getting a considered answer rather than a hasty brush-off from a busy shopkeeper it may be sensible to take some samples of your work with you; also, before asking advice, you should certainly check up on the kind of goods the shop already stocks and the sort of clientele it attracts—you can scarcely expect the shopkeeper to take you seriously if you have not taken the trouble to make sure that he does not already have a source of supply or that his customers are likely to want what you have to sell. You must also have some idea of how your goods are going to be priced.

Unless you are proposing to sell something unique or extremely unusual, you can also learn a lot from studying advertisements. If, for instance, you are looking for work as a decorator, a glance at the local paper and in the windows of local tobacconists' shops, etc will reveal what sort of competition you are up against—but do not jump to conclusions. A lack of advertisements may mean not that you are free from competition but that others have tried advertising and found no response. Conversely, the fact that a competitor advertises regularly and often probably means that he has found that he attracts customers by this means and that the prospects may be good for you. The same principle can be applied to trade and specialist journals; if a service or a product is regularly advertised by several different suppliers, this suggests that there is a demand for it.

There are also a great many factors which, though professional market researchers would dress them up in statistics and jargon, are really a matter of common sense. The kind of shops in your high street, the quality of goods they stock, and the levels of prices they charge; the evening courses offered at the local technical college or evening institute; the stock of books in the local library; the entries in your local Yellow Pages; these can all tell you a lot about your neighbourhood, the sort of people who live there, and the likelihood that they will want to buy what you hope to sell.

If your local grocers assume that 'coffee' means instant coffee and ham comes out of a can, then you may have difficulty interesting them in your home-made *pâté de foie aux truffes*. If your evening institute mainly offers classes in art appreciation, embroidery and Italian renaissance architecture then you can probably forget the course on spot welding which you had prepared and ditch your plan to sell cheap mail order goods to your neighbours. If there are three watchmakers with entries in the Yellow Pages you can reckon that the demand for watch and clock repairs is already being met.

With a little ingenuity you should be able to think of other, slightly more indirect, means of research. An antique dealer may well know if there is a local demand for someone who can repair china or restore furniture; a printer or stationer will know whether the demand for graphic design is being adequately met; a riding school will tell you if you would find customers for your skills as a saddler; if there is a need for an architect willing to take on small, spare-time jobs in the district the most likely people to be aware of it are local builders.

Even on a wider scale, supposing that yours is a product which needs more than a local market, it is possible to do some research fairly easily. The circulation of specialist journals and the numbers of members in societies or institutions will reveal something about the extent of public interest in a particular hobby or pursuit. You can even, at a fairly negligible cost, insert a small advertisement as an experiment to see what kind of response it brings for a service such as freelance typing or design. You can make enquiries in writing as well as face to face: tourist boards can tell you how many visitors your area attracts and the level of demand for accommodation; publishers will respond to ideas for books, or samples of articles; photographic agencies will let you know whether they are interested in marketing your pictures.

Sadly, as the example of the Ford Edsel showed, the best market research in the world cannot guarantee success; the Edsel was, when it was launched on the American market, the most thoroughly market-researched car ever. In theory everything about it was right—in practice the one thing that mattered was wrong. No one wanted it. It proved to be one of the most disastrous ventures in the history of the motor industry. But even the kind of elementary research suggested can provide a clear warning if you are being over-optimistic and, equally importantly, it can help you start off on the right foot. It may not be question of whether or not you should do this or make that, but of whether customers are going to want this done in a particular way, or whether they will buy that from a certain kind of shop. You are, in other words, testing not only whether there is a market for your product, but also whether the form in which you plan to offer it and the means by which you hope to sell it are appropriate.

Conclusion

Even when you have weighed up all the pros and cons which apply in your particular case and selected the source of spare-time income which best suits your situation, you will not, if you are prudent, plunge straight in at the deep end.

You will have done your 'looking before you leap' in the shape of the elementary market research suggested, but in many cases you will not have to leap at all but will be able to proceed slowly and cautiously. One of the nice things about the choice of spare-time income, as opposed to the choice of a career, is that you do not have to make a once-and-for-all commitment and if you find you have miscalculated or made a bad choice you can usually cut your losses before they become too severe.

None of this means that you should not start out with every morsel of enthusiasm you can muster—you will need it. What it does mean is that if, say, you have decided to start a carpentry business, you should not immediately invest in an armoury of power tools and buy up a timber yard. Begin, if you can, with the minimum of equipment and buy materials as you need them. It may involve improvisation, and even some waste of time and money, but it will enable you to get the feeling of the work, assess your needs in the light of experience and reassure your-self that the project is a viable one without gambling your life savings. As you gather momentum and confidence you can speed up, buy more tools, lay in stocks of materials and plan ahead safe in the knowledge that work will come your way and that you know how to cope with it.

2. Selling Yourself, Your Product or Service

Clearly, there is no space in this book to provide instructions on how to make a range of goods from pies to pots and pinafores, or how to perform services as various as playgroups and proofreading, but they do all have one thing in common—they have to be sold. Even if your choice of source for earning money from home boils down to finding casual or part-time employment, you are going to have to sell yourself when you apply for a job; and if you have decided to work for yourself, producing goods for sale or offering your skills as a freelance in the market-place, then selling yourself is not going to be a matter of a single interview or application, but a constant and crucial process.

Basic PR

Selling yourself is the first step towards selling your goods or services. No one is going to employ you to paint their house if you live in something which looks like a casualty of the hurricane, or ask you to keep their books of account if you can't remember their telephone number. There is no point in trying to disguise the fact that yours is a spare-time business; but equally, a first priority must be to convince your customers that this does not mean it is a sloppy, unreliable or amateurish one.

Have proper letterheads and business cards printed, even if they carry no more than your name and address—with small print shops blossoming in every high street the cost of getting these designed and printed is surprisingly little. If at all possible, type your correspondence; for one thing it is going to make the essential business of keeping copies a lot easier, and even if the information conveyed is exactly the same, a neatly typed letter with a printed heading instils far more confidence than the same letter scrawled on a mauve sheet from a writing pad, or a page from a duplicate book.

If your business is going to involve a lot of telephone calls then do make sure that other members of the family are trained to deal with them. A customer who rings up to enquire about the advertisement you put in the paper last week will quickly lose interest if he finds himself talking to a ten-year-old who can only say that 'Dad's out and I don't know when he'll be back', while the telly bellows in the background. On the other hand, a courteous request for name and number and a promise that the call will be returned at a given time might well result in business. If your phone is going to be unattended for long periods you should probably invest in an answering machine. Just because your spare-time work is something that you do after 6.00 pm, this does not mean that all your customers want to talk to you in the evening. Do not try and get round this by conducting your spare-time work from your employer's office. Not only could you find yourself with more spare time than you want, but it will inevitably lead to misunderstandings, lost messages and muddle.

Though you may feel that you are at an enormous disadvantage in competing with large, full-time businesses, you do have one incalculable quality on your side: you are an individual. Large organisations go to vast trouble and expense to portray themselves as friendly, caring, cosy people you can sit down and have a chat with—inventing a 'lovable' figure like Buzby (remember him?) or paying well-known personalities to project an image which disguises the fact that they are really vast, anonymous businesses which cannot possibly lend a sympathetic ear to every customer's complaint or accommodate particular needs. But if Mrs Smith has just noticed that the lovely vase you sold her has a chip on the base, or if one of your bed and breakfast guests prefers tea to coffee, you don't have to call the manager to authorise a credit note or brusquely say that tea is 'off'; you can exchange the vase or brew the tea and your customers will happily tell each other how pleasant it is to deal with you, rather than the department store or the hotel chain.

In short, you have no choice but to give that 'personal service' which larger businesses have to struggle to provide. What you must not do is leap to the conclusion that individuality and personal contact can make up for inefficiency and bad quality. If you always give a sweet to the children who come with their parents to buy your hand-made toys you will be considered charmingly eccentric; if you never have the toy they want in stock and the kids get covered in paint which has not had time to dry properly, you may still be eccentric but you will not charm anybody. Make a point of always keeping appointments, always delivering things when you say you will, giving accurate estimates and sticking to them, answering letters by return and dealing with queries or complaints politely and generously.

What goes for your customers goes for your suppliers too. As a business, even a part-time one, you may be entitled to credit or better terms than are available to private customers. But, in exchange, you must behave like a business, to know what you want and to order it properly. Your custom may be worth more than that of the casual shopper, but it will cease to be worthwhile to your suppliers if you are always wanting to exchange goods or if they can never read the handwriting on your orders.

Selling your product

There are many different ways of getting your product to the customer, but they break down into three main categories:

- Selling direct, ie the customer comes to you or you go to him
- Selling through an intermediary in the form of a retailer or wholesaler
- Selling by mail.

Selling direct

If you are selling a service then this is almost certainly the method you will be adopting, though in a few cases, like home typing work, there may be an intermediary in the form of an agency. The great advantage of dealing with your customers face to face, so to speak, is that the full price of your product goes to you. A retailer or wholesaler naturally expects to receive a discount, and selling by mail, as we shall see, is generally an expensive business. The corresponding disadvantage is that you can find yourself devoting so much time to selling that you have very little left to perform the service or make the goods concerned. Less obvious drawbacks are that you may also have to spend a great deal more time on paperwork if you are coping with a multiplicity of small sales and that you may be running a greater risk, if yours is a business which involves you in extending credit.

There can be no doubt that the most potent selling weapon in the armoury of the majority of spare-time businesses is word-of-mouth recommendation. Anyone is more likely to follow the recommendation of a relation, friend, neighbour or colleague at work who has discovered 'this wonderful accountant/electrician/bed and breakfast place/*pâté de campagne*' than to respond to an advertisement or brochure, however lavish and expensive. This is where your personal PR effort, already discussed, will pay off; it may be that your product is little better or cheaper than its competitors, but the person who is giving the recommendation has had personal contact with *you*; he feels he has been clever in finding you, and he feels important by virtue of having this exciting discovery to pass on.

If you are selling direct then your sales effort is likely to concentrate on your immediate locality—gourmets are not going to trek up from Somerset to sample your Eccles cakes, nor do you want to undertake a rewiring job that involves a two-hour drive each way. There are exceptions, naturally: if your service is very specialised or in some way unique then you may be trying to reach a much wider market geographically, but it is also likely that the clientele you are seeking is limited in some other way, by interest or occupation, for example. Thus a spare-time decorator might get all the work he wants through a classified advertisement in a local paper with a circulation of ten thousand. A craftsman who specialises in repairing enamelled snuffboxes might get the same results by advertising in a specialist magazine with an even smaller circulation. In neither case would a full-page advertisement in, say, *Radio Times* reach a greater number of potential customers.

Assume for the moment that your sales effort is a local one. Your efforts will be concentrated on reaching those local people who are potential clients for your service or customers for your goods. If your product is one that has a general market—suppose you simply have rooms to let, or are producing toddlers' clothes or repairing electrical appliances— then the local newspaper, cards in the window of newsagents or leaflets through the letter-box will be your main opportunities for advertising. If you can achieve the same effect at no cost by persuading the paper to write up your toddlers' garments, then all the better. But if you are selling some more specialised product—your accountancy services, a booklet on local history, or your watercolours of local views—then try to think of ways and means of reaching the people who are most likely to be interested. Will the local Chamber of Commerce or National Farmers' Union branch give you a membership list? Perhaps the local library would display a poster for your booklet? There may be an art society which would send out a leaflet on your pictures with its newsletter, or the technical college may run evening classes where a poster could be displayed. Had you thought of trying your toys on neighbourhood playgroups? Maybe the antique shop will keep a supply of leaflets advertising your china repair service?

Selling is not a matter of buying a pair of shoes with steel toecaps and looking for doorways in which to stick them. You are aiming to build up a reputation and a regular clientele. So when the first customer does call up or knocks at the door, don't fall on him like an evangelical preacher on a drunkard; do not, on the other hand, behave as if you were doing him a favour. Explain what you can—and just as important, what you can't—offer, honestly and fairly; when he asks about prices, don't look as if you were embarrassed at the mention of money, but don't try to pretend you are offering the bargain of the century either. The good salesman is the one who inspires trust and who convinces the customer that both parties are going to get a fair deal.

Selling through retailers or wholesalers

It is unlikely that many spare-time businesses will produce on a scale sufficient to justify dealing through a wholesaler. The exceptions tend to occur if you produce goods on contract, in which case they are probably sold under someone else's name or brand name. Say, for example, you assemble garments for the 'rag trade' or fancy goods for a stationery manufacturer. In this case, your selling problem boils down to getting the contract; and whether the goods move out of the shop is none of your concern.

But if you do hit upon a line which necessitates wholesale distribution most of what follows about selling to retailers will apply to you. The differences are that your life is simplified in that you only have to deal with one or two accounts, but your profit is reduced because the wholesaler has to keep something for himself, and needs a bigger discount than the retailer.

When you sell through a retailer rather than direct to the

consumer you are taking advantage of the fact that he has a shop with regular customers and a passing trade who will be interested in your goods. You are also passing on to the shop-keeper the risk you took, in time and money, when you manu-factured the goods. If he buys them from you and cannot sell them to his customers that is his problem. In exchange, you are selling him the goods at a discount, ie for less than you would get if you sold them direct to the consumer.

The first thing to establish is the range of discounts which is current in your particular line. The variation can be enormous, with retailers taking a margin as low as 15 per cent and as high as 50 per cent. The level will depend mainly upon the kind of goods they trade in. Food shops, for instance, work upon fairly low discounts because they sell their goods quickly; at the other end of the range, a bookshop stocks a vast number of different items which sell fairly slowly, and so requires a large discount. But other factors come into the equation. Large stores and supermarkets work on small margins, relying on their high vol-ume of trade to make up for a lower profit per unit, whereas small corner shops need to have a larger margin to survive.

Being your own rep

Let us take a concrete example in the matronly shape of Mrs Barlow. Mrs B's pork pies had made her something of a local cel-ebrity: they were always in demand for charity bazaars, the foodstall at the village fete, etc. So many people told her how much they wished there was somewhere they could buy 'a good old-fashioned pie like this' that she began to wonder whether they might not be the source of additional income. But though her pies were famous in Clay-in-the-Wold where she lives, the population is only 453 and it was clear that it would have a lim-ited appetite for pies, even Mrs B's. She would have to break into the larger market of nearby Woldingham, where she and her pies were unknown.

Investigation showed that the best grocer in Woldingham High Street sold only mass-produced, cellophane-wrapped pies which, a quick consumer test on Mr Barlow confirmed, were not a patch on Mrs B's. But they sold at £1.20 each and the grocer said that, while he'd be delighted to try Mrs B's pies, he had to make a 20 per cent margin on his cold meat counter. In other words, he pocketed 24p each time he sold one of those cello-phane-wrapped horrors.

Mrs B reckoned the citizens of Woldingham would be happy to pay an extra 20p for the quality she offered. If she gave the grocer a 20 per cent discount then, out of the £1.40 which the consumer paid, he would get 28p and she would keep £1.12. She had already done her costings (see page 80) and saw that, provided she could sell 100 pies a week, that price would produce a worthwhile income for her.

The problem was that the grocer, though he was keen to try Mrs B's pies on his customers, couldn't possibly sell more than 25 a week. Mrs B set out, with some samples in her bag, to find other customers. Despite a good many failures—the department store couldn't cope with a specialist line like hers, the baker already made his own pies, the supermarket wouldn't dream of it unless she could give them a price under 80p—she got enough outlets willing to give her pies a chance. They were not all retailers; a couple of pubs liked the look of them and gave her an order for half a dozen each, a restaurant agreed to try them out on their cold buffet, and the lady who ran the Women's Institute stall at the town's weekly market was sure she could sell half a dozen.

But Mrs B realised that, although the grocer would almost certainly encourage his customers to try her pies, some of the other shops were not really convinced that they would sell, the Italian delicatessen, for example. With Latin gallantry Franco, the proprietor, had agreed to take six pies but the chances were that he would hide them away behind the pizza, which was infuriating because Mrs B knew that his prosperous middle-class customers were exactly the kind of people who could and would pay a bit extra for quality. Moreover, she was convinced that there were other shops which had made a mistake in turning her away. It was not enough, she realised, to sell the pies to the shops, she had to help the shopkeepers, even against their better judgement, to sell them to the consumer.

What Mrs B did was to go back and take further advantage of that charming young Italian. She cajoled him into putting her pies right at the front of the counter, with a card on top, provided by her, announcing them as 'Traditional Clay-in-the-Wold Hand-Raised Pork Pies'. He doubled his order the next week. Then she found that, at a cost of only a penny a pie, she could have paper wrappings printed with the same wording and a picture of a contented-looking pig and her name and address. Soon several of the shops which turned her down in the first place were asking if they could buy her pies too. The point was that now, when people followed the grocer's recommendation and tried one of the pies, they could easily discover that what they were enjoying was not just a very good pork pie, but one of *Mrs Barlow's* pork pies. They soon asked their local grocers why they did not stock them, and some even made the pilgrimage to Clay-in-the-Wold to get more. Mrs B was careful, despite her euphoria, to make sure that the shopkeepers who backed her in the beginning always got all the pies they wanted, even if the Johnny-come-latelies had to go short—they had backed her, now she was in a position to show her appreciation.

Moreover, Mrs B did not just stay at home and bake pies, but made a point of visiting her customers at regular intervals, discussing their orders and listening to any complaints about the quality or delivery. She could be firm. When she found that one of the pubs always found a reason for delaying payment of her account, she simply put her foot down and insisted on cash on delivery; on the other hand, when Franco at the delicatessen had to shut the shop for a week because his wife was rushed to hospital, Mrs B instantly took his quota of pies back and sold them elsewhere. She always had time for a cup of tea with her customers and a glass—'well, just a *little* one'—of Chianti with Franco. She warned her customers when she and Mr Barlow were going away on a fortnight's holiday, so that they were prepared for a break in supplies. She listened to their suggestions, too, and as a result of one from Franco she is building up a promising line of 'Olde Woldingham Game Pies'. Finally, she never has sold a pie to the supermarket. The manager came begging on her doorstep, offering an order for a hundred pies a week. But she asked some sharp questions and found out that he planned to sell the pies at £1.10 as a 'loss leader'. If that happened, Mrs B saw, he would take all the custom away from her regular shops, and once he had cornered the market, he would be in a position to dictate to her the price at which she sold, or he might just cancel the order to make room for the cheese promotion his area manager was planning.

In fact, Mrs Barlow worked out for herself most of the principles of effective marketing and of how to be a good 'rep'. She sought out not just the obvious outlets for her goods, but also the less obvious. She was not satisfied with simply selling into the shops, but offered help and advice in selling the goods to their customers. She made sure that her product had a clear identity, so that it would be asked for by name. When it came to calling on her customers, she was politely tough with those who behaved badly, but stood loyally by those who supported her; she kept them informed if their supplies were going to be affected; she did not succumb to the temptation to make a quick killing with the supermarket, but realised that her long-term advantage lay with her regular outlets. Above all, perhaps, her customers liked Mrs B and came to look forward to her regular calls.

The lessons for any business, spare-time or full-time, are plain. If you plan to go calling on shopkeepers and persuading them to try stocking your produce, there are a few simple rules to remember.

- Have a proper order pad or duplicate book, so that you can write down their order and give them a copy; if they quote an order number then write that down too, and of course the price upon which you have agreed. If they ask for a particular delivery date, then stick to it.

- Make your calls regularly, but not too frequently. The shopkeeper may be delighted to see you once a month or once a quarter, but if you drop in every other day to check if he has sold one of those stuffed toys you delivered on Tuesday, you will cease being a welcome visitor and become a nuisance. Remember, too, that you are not more but less important than the customers. If the man behind the counter of the craft shop keeps five customers waiting while you show him your hand-painted vases, he is losing trade, and probably taking a heartfelt dislike to you and your vases. It is up to you to find out when it is likely to suit each particular buyer to see you, and to make sure that when he does you are ready and prepared to display your wares and make your case as succinctly as possible.

- Do not try to tell a shopkeeper his business, nor press a sale when a customer is really reluctant. It is useless telling a gift shop owner that your vases are based on a third century Greek original and that you did a two-year course as the Royal Academy of Arts if his stock-in-trade is plastic toby jugs and souvenir dishcloths. You may feel that he should raise the cultural tone of his business, but he knows that his main source of custom is the coachloads of trippers who would consider a pot of classical purity a poor thing when compared with a pink one inscribed 'A Present from the Pennines'. On the other hand, the little art gallery across the square attracts quite a different kind of customer and could probably sell some vases if you provided them with a tasteful showcard setting out the vases' ancestry and your impressive qualifications, especially if you persuaded them to display a couple as an experiment and agreed to take them back if it did not work.

Selling from stalls

If you do not have the time or the inclination to sell your goods through shops, or if your pricing does not allow for the discounts they require, you can look at the possibility of selling direct to your customers from a market stall, or even in some instances, attracting a passing trade to your own home.

Most street markets are controlled by the local authority, which issues licences to traders, regulates the kinds of goods that may be sold, etc. In the case of other markets, the owners of the site will operate a similar system, charging a fee for stall space and making sure that individual stallholders obey local bylaws, health regulations and so forth. Enquiries at the market you have in mind will point you in the right direction and enable you to contact the appropriate person. But remember that there may well be a waiting list, and established stallholders may have some say, official or unofficial, when it comes to admitting newcomers who would compete with them. You should also take account of the fact that, though a market is a temporary affair, operating perhaps only one day a week, each stallholder has a regular pitch and an established clientele. There is little point in hiring a stall and turning up at the market only three or four times a year. A much more likely prospect for a spare-time business is some form of co-operative effort with people in a similar position, or an arrangement to sell your goods from an established stall. You will have to be prepared, of course, to give up some proportion of your takings to cover the costs of the co-operative stall, or to make it worthwhile for a stallholder to give you space, but the overheads of a market trader are, obviously, a good deal lower than those of a shopkeeper and the percentage you have to give up should be proportionately less. In some markets local bodies such as the

Women's Institute have regular stalls for the sale of members' produce, and this may be an opening well worth some investigation.

What about a roadside stall, or a sign directing passing drivers to your home? Provided that you are not causing traffic problems by blocking the by-pass or setting up shop on the local accident black spot, police and local authorities will probably tolerate any technical breach of bylaws, etc. But, if your neighbours find that your customers' cars are taking up their usual parking spot, or that their children are littering the street with sweet papers, they may reasonably object. Whether it is a worthwhile effort depends entirely on circumstances which only you can judge. If you are fortunate enough to live in the Lake District, then a sign offering local handicrafts, delicacies or whatever may bring a steady trade from tourists with time on their hands and money to spend. A similar sign in a Liverpool housing estate is unlikely to get results. 'Bed and Breakfast, first right at the Windmill' sounds tempting; 'Bed and Breakfast, second left at the steel works' does not.

Selling by mail

There are two principal ways of using the postal service to sell your goods. The first, mail order proper, involves sending out brochures or leaflets to households or particular individuals, inviting them to order your goods by using an order form which is incorporated in your selling material. The second, direct response advertising, means placing advertisements in the media which again incorporate some sort of order form or coupon. The advantages of both methods of selling are that you are presenting your goods to the consumers in their own homes, rather than in a crowded shop, and offering them a way of acting immediately if they decide to buy. In theory at least, you are also offering a better price because you are cutting out the middle man in the form of the shopkeeper. Some shopkeepers feel strongly about this, so if you intend to sell by mail as well as through shops, try to ensure that the two do not conflict and that you are not selling to the shops with one hand and undercutting their price with the other. Because mail order involves selling direct to large numbers of individuals whose credit-worthiness is unknown and who may live at the other end of the country, it is almost always done on a cash-with-order basis. This, of course, is good for the sellers' cash flow since you get the money before the goods leave your hands.

The disadvantages of both forms of selling by mail are the cost and the risk. With mail order a lavish piece of sales literature has to be produced (with so much lush colour printing arriving through the post, trying to produce a brochure on the cheap is almost certainly a false economy), and mailed to several hundred or thousand addresses. In the case of direct response advertising, you have to design and pay for a striking advertisement as well as satisfying the stringent conditions of the newspapers' Mail Order Protection Scheme. Either of these items requires sufficient capital outlay to prevent you offering bargain basement prices. But you also have to allow for the fact that, with mail order, you may have to include a reply paid envelope (the Post Office can provide information about freepost rates, etc) and you will also have to include the cost of posting the goods in your price or add 'p&p' on as an extra. These considerations mean that selling by mail can only be employed for fairly expensive items or for goods or services which involve continuing sales: magazine subscriptions, book clubs, etc. No one is going to send off for something that costs only a couple of pounds if they have to pay £1.50 postage and packing as well.

Large organisations offering goods with universal appeal, such as clothes, luggage or the *Reader's Digest*, find it worthwhile to use direct response advertisements or direct mail on the scattergun principle, taking space in the Sunday colour magazines or mailing to every household in Manchester. But you must bear in mind that even they, with enormous experience to call on, the most sophisticated sales literature and, probably, mouth-watering special offers to sweeten the pill, count themselves lucky if their 'response rate' (ie the percentage of those seeing the offer who actually respond) is as high as 2 per cent. Anyway, supposing any spare-time business could afford the initial cost of such an approach, it is very unlikely that it would have, or could quickly provide, the stocks of goods to meet even a poor response. The only case where a scattergun approach may be appropriate is locally. The Post Office will quote prices for delivering literature to particular areas in your district; or if the kids constantly complain that they are 'bored', why not send them out with a stack of leaflets to put through letter boxes? Provided that what you are offering is of fairly general interest this could pay off, but it is almost certainly pointless strewing the entire council estate with information about your hand-made quilts or the old people's flats with details of your ballet classes.

For most spare-time businesses considering selling by mail, the carefully aimed shot is more appropriate than the scatter-gun. To reach those people, and only those people, who are pre-disposed to be interested in what you are selling saves time and money, and you can also write your copy and design your advertisement especially for them. Suppose you make superb split-cane fly-fishing rods. If you send a leaflet about them to every male between 15 and 50 in Yorkshire then you are wasting an awful lot of paper and postage on the ones who can't tell a trout from a turbot, and have no interest in either unless it's on a plate and surrounded by chips. But if you can get hold of the membership list of the Yorkshire Fly-fishing Society, you only need a hundredth as many leaflets and you can safely get straight down to the nitty-gritty of explaining that your rod is the ideal one for casting a double-tapered, floating line up-stream, etc.

Somewhere, in some form, there is almost certainly a list of names and addresses covering every interest, business, society and activity known to man — the problem is how to get hold of it. There are, of course, professional mailing organisations which will either do mailings for you or sell their lists of names and addresses, usually in the form of printed labels. But such services are expensive, and very often not kept fully up to date. They also naturally tend to concentrate on areas of general rather than specialist interest. Clubs and societies are an obvious source, but must be approached with circumspection. The secretary of the Townswomen's Guild knows she is not going to be popular if she gives a membership list to the local sex shop. Other businesses in the same field may be willing to sell their mailing lists, though they are likely to be cautious — the effectiveness of a list diminishes with use. One thing any business which regularly produces leaflets or other literature should do is to keep a file of the names and addresses of those who have purchased or enquired about its product. Building your own mailing list takes time, but is the best long-term solution.

An alternative, often a cheaper one, to obtaining mailing lists is to advertise in specialist journals. You get the same benefit of reaching only those you want to reach, and whereas a mailing shot is something which gets an instant reaction, a magazine will be studied at leisure. The leaflet extolling your fishing rods may land on the breakfast table of Mr Dale, the enthusiastic Yorkshire trout fisherman, just as he's coming to terms with a hangover and his electricity bill; chances are he'll toss it in the fire. But he will see your advertisement in *Trout and Salmon* that evening when he's sitting with his feet up and daydreaming about the coming season and how it really is time he treated himself to a new rod.

A useful book on the subject is *Running Your Own Mail Order Business* (Kogan Page).

Selling a service

Services, like goods, can be sold through intermediaries—in the form of agents—or direct by personal contact or by mail. The same basic principles apply.

An agent can serve two purposes. First, in the case of work like home typing or office cooking, an agency provides the means by which your customer finds you and saves you the donkey work of going out and drumming up business. Second, if you are selling something like photographs or literary work, where prices can be almost infinitely variable, an agent can ensure that you get the best possible price for your work—it is his job to know the market, understand that one magazine with a circulation in the hundreds of thousands can afford to pay top rates whereas another, struggling along with a few thousand readers, cannot.

As a means of finding work, an agent can be a necessary intermediary; as a guide and handholder in the commercial jungle he may be a vital ally. But in either capacity he will be worse than useless if he is inefficient, or doesn't know his job. Customers will go out of their way to avoid an agency whose arrangements always collapse in chaos or which supplies them with incompetent workers or offers potential employees inappropriate work. If you get on the books of such an agency, not only will you get less work than you could, but you will also find yourself tarred with their bad reputation. So, if at all possible, always check on an agency's standing and reputation before asking them to represent you.

In nearly every case, of course, an agency makes its living by taking a commission out of your earnings—you are paying them to work for you and have a right to expect good service and integrity. The world being what it is, you cannot automatically assume that you will get it. It is therefore prudent, if at all feasible, to check up with one or more of the agency's established clients. The need for this is particularly important if the agency is going to be collecting fees on your behalf; it is not, alas, totally unknown for agents of the smaller, fly-by-night kind to have a brief spree at their client's expense. You should also check that the rate of commission the agent charges is not excessive. Rates vary so greatly from industry to industry that no hard and fast rules can be given, but the minimum will certainly be 10 per cent and the maximum, in the case of art galleries for example, may be up to 50 per cent.

One other difference between the selling of goods and the selling of services is worth emphasising. Though in both cases the customer will be influenced most of all by quality and value, in the case of a service a lot may depend on your own personality. A customer buying your dresses by mail order does not give a hoot whether you are an habitual grump and a vicious gossip, but if she is coming to your house for a fitting she probably won't come back a second time if she gets her head bitten off or hears her best friend comprehensively slandered. On the other hand, customers will often put up with a surprising degree of inefficiency or with high prices if they like the person they are dealing with.

However you sell your products or services, the process may, and in some cases must, be backed up by three complementary processes: advertising, publicity or promotion, and distribution.

Advertising
Press advertising falls into two categories, classified and display. Classified advertisements are set by the paper or magazine in a standard form and grouped together under general headings such as 'For Sale', 'Wanted', etc. You normally pay by the word or by the line. Display advertisements are designed by the advertiser who usually supplies the paper with 'camera ready copy' — an exact facsimile of the advertisement as it will appear, ready to be photographed by the printer. The cost of display advertisements is related to the space they take up, usually expressed as the number of columns or fractions of a column in newspapers and as fractions of a page in a magazine — for example, ten column centimetres will be a space one column wide and ten centimetres deep; a half double column is two columns wide

and half the page in depth. You may also be able to specify within limits where you want the advertisement to appear, but you could have to pay a premium for 'solus' space (no other advertisements adjoining yours) or for special positions like the back cover or contents page of a magazine. All publications which carry advertising will supply on request a rate card specifying their current rates, and the information is collected in that ad man's Bible, *British Rate and Data* (published monthly and annually by BRAD, Maclean Hunter House, Chalk Lane, Cockfosters, Barnet, Herts EN4 0BD).

Classified advertising is relatively easy in that all you have to provide is the wording, but display advertising demands both a designer's skill and the services of a typesetter (a few papers will still set display advertisements for you, but the choice of type will be limited). To try to design your own advertisements, unless you have a real flair for it, is to be penny wise and pound foolish; if in any doubt go to a freelance designer, and it may well be sensible to employ someone to write the copy for you too.

The rates charged by different media will depend mainly upon their circulation and, to a lesser extent, on what the professionals call the 'quality' of that circulation. In other words, *The Plutocrat's Gazette*, whose readership, by definition, has money to burn, can charge more per reader than the *Pauper's Press*. Remember too that readership can be a very different thing from circulation; a monthly magazine may be working its way round the household while the daily paper is in the dustbin wrapped round the leftover fish and chips.

Any advertiser, on however small a scale, can learn one thing from the big boys: advertising works cumulatively. A single advertisement can be missed by many readers, and will be ignored by many others, but if it is repeated for four weeks, or in six monthly issues, it will sooner or later catch the eye of most of them. So, however tempted you are to splurge your entire advertising budget on half a page in the journal of your choice, think twice. The same money might buy you six half columns. Not only will these, overall, be seen and noted by far more customers, but the response will be spread over a period so that you get a steady flow of orders rather than a sudden surge which may well stretch your resources. Most papers will give a 'series discount' for both classified and display bookings.

The most likely advertising media for the spare-time business are local or regional newspapers and specialist magazines.

Though newspapers may take bookings at short notice (in the case of their classified columns, as little as 24 hours), magazines tend to have long lead times, and you should book well ahead, especially if you want your advertisement to get a good position. If you have a choice of media, then it is sensible to try some experiments: if you are asking for direct responses, then make sure you can distinguish from which newspaper or magazine each coupon came, keep a running total of the responses from each and, by relating the number of responses to the cost of space, compare the cost-effectiveness of each advertisement.

Unlike a detergent manufacturer or a brewer, the spare-time business cannot simply exhort people to 'Buy Gleam' or 'Drink Tarzan—the Macho Lager'. You not only have to persuade people to want your goods, you have to tell them how or where to get them. Always include your address as well as your name, even if you are not incorporating a reply coupon in the advertisement. If you are distributing your wares through shops, then tell them when and where you are going to advertise. Even if they don't order more in anticipation of extra demand, at least you have shown them that you are spending money to help them sell your product. You can also suggest that, in return for a contribution towards the cost of the advertisement, you will include them in a list of stockists. Such co-operative advertising can benefit both parties.

Above all, do not try and be too clever. The Guinness toucan may have been vastly successful, but it took years and millions of pounds to establish it in the public's mind. You are better off with straightforward, clearly designed advertisements which say what you have to sell, why people should buy it and how they can obtain it.

Promotion and publicity

Promotion is offering a week's holiday in the Bahamas to the first person who can collect three box tops and put the five qualities of a 'superwife' in the right order; promotion is the rather disconsolate chap dressed up as Sir Lancelot giving away free samples of 'Guinevere' scent in the department store; publicity is taking the man who writes the 'Freewheel' column out to a liquid lunch and persuading him that he should give a plug to your new economy product.

You will probably not have to do any of these things to earn your extra money from home, but you can apply the same principles on your very much humbler levels. You can create an identity for your product, you can bring it to people's attention or persuade them to try it, you can get yourself or your goods written about in the papers.

Packaging, for instance, need not be a very expensive business, but it can make all the difference to your sales. If you are making, let us say, decorative jewellery, then if you simply sell the brooches, earrings and bracelets individually, they are going to end up as loose items in a drawer or display case. But if you make them up into sets fixed to something as elementary as a piece of card with your name and address printed on it, then the shop has an opportunity of displaying them, the customers will be buying a set rather than a single item, and they will know who made them and where to go for more. This last is a crucial point and even if your product is one that cannot easily be packaged you should try to make sure that it carries your name somewhere.

You can also offer shops, where appropriate, some simple form of display material. Cardboard mountings or showcards can be manufactured relatively cheaply and may make all the difference between stock languishing under the counter or getting a place in the window.

If a local charity is running a bazaar, why not offer a few of your goods as a contribution to one of the stalls or a prize in the raffle? Perhaps you could have a stand, or share one, at the county show; there may be ways in which you can take advantage of events like local festivals by getting shops to promote your goods. Everything and anything can be grist to the promotional mill.

The vital point to remember about publicity is that you have got to give value for money. In other words, if you want the media to give you free publicity then you have got to give them a story. Your photograph is not going to get into the local paper just because your pottery or your ballet classes are the best of their kind. But if you win an award for your pots or if your ex-pupil becomes prima ballerina at Sadler's Wells, then that is a story.

Finally, your part-time business almost certainly makes you, at some level, an expert on something. Someone has got to fill the space around your advertisement in that specialist magazine, why not you? You are not only promoting your product and spreading your reputation, you are actually being paid to do it. Any one of the local societies or institutions in your area may be searching for speakers for their meetings, and the evening institute may be looking for someone to give courses on your subject. Why not offer your services?

Distribution

All your effort in selling, advertising, promotion and publicity will be wasted if customers cannot get your products when they want them. Worse, it will create positive ill-will if you create a demand which you cannot meet. You will not be able to get your produce into every shop in the district, so try to make sure that if the local paper does a story about you they also tell the readers where to find you or your wares. And that will be wasted if the shops concerned don't have them in stock; if you have persuaded a shopkeeper to sell your goods you have moved forward one square, but you go back two when you cannot supply his needs.

If your business is local, then physically distributing the goods to your customers will probably depend on making the best use of your car, taking advantage of shopping expeditions, etc. But do not underrate the time and money involved. A little forethought can ensure that you do not waste two hours in a traffic jam delivering £5 worth of goods.

If your customers are further afield then you will probably be using the Post Office; again, planning can avoid waste. For instance a couple of parcels which the clerk would deal with in five minutes during a quiet period may waste an hour first thing on Monday morning when pensioners and other claimants are besieging the counter. Do make sure that your parcels are fully insured—the Post Office has relatively cheap schemes, but you can also ask your insurance company about a policy which covers you against loss or damage to goods in transit. A possible alternative to the mail is British Rail's 'Red Star' service, which is reliable and fast, but also fairly costly. For large packages you may also consider using one of the private road transport firms.

Once you have put your goods in the hands of the carrier there is nothing you can do but hope; before that, though, you can do your bit to speed up the process by ensuring that orders are dealt with promptly and goods dispatched by return. Efficiency in this respect will cost you little and may gain you much in terms of good-will, repeat business and reputation.

Getting part-time employment

If your choice of work boils down to finding a spare-time job on someone else's payroll, then the same rules apply as to any other form of job-seeking. In a written application or at an interview, stress those qualifications or qualities which fit you for the job, appear confident but don't try to bluff a prospective employer too far. Tailor your manner and appearance to the occasion. If, for example, you are applying for a job as an attendant on a garage forecourt in the evenings, you will not strengthen your case by turning up in a lounge suit and carrying the attaché case you use in your daytime work as a sales representative, or by telling the proprietor that his display of soft drinks is badly arranged. When he has reassured himself that you can work a petrol pump and balance the till, he may well be interested in your ideas—but right now what he needs to do is fill the gap left by Mike who suddenly decided to take evening classes in disco dancing.

Get things straight right at the outset by establishing how many hours you are going to be expected to work, what you will be paid for them and exactly what you are going to have to do. Part-timers can easily become the dogsbodies around any workplace. If you have been hired to do the washing-up in a restaurant kitchen, you must expect to cope with a lot of dirty crockery, but if you have been employed as the cook for the directors' dining room there is no reason why you should wash up coffee cups for the entire secretarial staff.

You must also make sure that the relationship between your full-time job and your spare-time one is clear to all parties. If, for example, your daytime employer has first call on your evenings for overtime, then you have got to make this clear to someone who is thinking of hiring you for evening work. Compromises are often possible, but only if everyone knows and understands the ground rules. Again, a local solicitor may be delighted to find that you, a qualified legal typist, can spare him three hours each evening, but if you don't tell him that you also work during the day in the police station both your employers will have cause for concern—you might be going straight from typing evidence for the prosecution to typing the brief for the defence.

Above all, do be clear about your relationship with the Inland Revenue. If you expect your part-time employer to pay you in crisp fivers and keep mum you are asking him to run a very big risk (see Chapter 4). You may consider that a nod and a wink covers the case, but anyone who has tried nodding and winking at one of Her Majesty's Inspectors of Taxes will know that the response tends to be very chilly indeed.

When it comes to actually finding job opportunities, the best place to look is probably your local paper. But more part-time jobs are found through personal contact and local knowledge than advertisements. Put it around your friends that you are seeking evening or weekend work; if you notice that the pub round the corner is short of a barmaid, or hear that Mrs So-and-So is having to give up her secretarial work at the old people's home, then ask. But do choose the right time and place: a landlord will not want to discuss terms and conditions in front of the whole saloon bar.

3. You're in Business

This chapter is intended mainly for those whose choice of spare-time work involves starting their own business, on however modest a scale, and can safely be skipped if you will be working for others in exchange for a wage. There are a number of essential differences between being employed, even part-time, and working for yourself. Though you may be doing exactly the same kind of work, your position changes when you come home at 5.30, have a cup of tea, give up for the day your job as Buildright & Co's painter and paper-hanger and start working on your own account as John Smith, Painter and Paper-hanger.

If, between 9.00 am and 5.00 pm, you misunderstand Mrs Jones's instructions and paint her bedroom ceiling puce, Buildright will have to appease Mrs Jones and pay for putting things right. If Buildright's estimate didn't allow for the fact that the red flock paper which has to be stripped from the stairwell is attached with superglue and you spend three hours' overtime getting it off, then they will have to adjust their price (if they can), pay you the overtime, and deduct PAYE. But if these things happen when you are working on your own account, *you* are going to have to soothe Mrs Jones, break the news that her bill is going up by £50, and remember to declare the additional income to the taxman after deducting the cost of the ten coats of white paint needed to cover the puce ceiling and the solvent needed to shift the superglue.

Once you decide to work on your own account in a regular, organised way you are, however modestly, starting a business. This will affect you in two ways: first, it means that the outside world—your customers and suppliers, the authorities and the law—are entitled to expect you to follow proper business practices, and to accept the restrictions, obligations and laws which apply to all businesses. Second, if you are going to run a business, then it will clearly benefit from being run in a business-like way. This does not mean that you have to enrol at the Harvard Business School or talk knowledgeably about discounted cash flow and inter-company balances. What it does mean is that you need to know and understand enough about the running of a business to make sure that yours is working to your maximum advantage.

Types of business

A small business can have three principal kinds of legal status: a sole trader, a partnership and a limited liability company.

A sole trader

In this case the individual and the business are legally and financially inseparable. If, for example, you undertake to mow your neighbour's lawn for a fee, you may call yourself Arcadia Landscape Services and print letterheads or open a bank account in that name. But the taxman will treat the fees you have received as part of your personal income, and will demand his share of what is left after you have deducted those costs which are allowable (see Chapter 4). Moreover, if you cut down your neighbour's prize dahlias in the process he can sue you, Joe Bloggs, for the damage and can, in the last resort, have not just your lawn-mower, but also Mrs Bloggs' diamond necklace, sold to satisfy his claim.

A partnership

A partnership is more complicated in that it has, in certain respects, an existence separate from that of the individual partners. A partnership must, for instance, draw up a set of accounts each year showing the profit or loss it has made from its activities; but those accounts will also show how that profit or loss has been divided among the partners and what monies they have paid into or withdrawn from the partnership during the year. In other words, a partnership is a common pool to which each partner contributes, but at any given moment the net value of the partnership can always be divided up between the partners in proportion to their participation. If, to come back to the lawn-mowing business, Arcadia Landscape Services is a partnership between you and your best friend to which you have each contributed £50 to buy a lawn-mower, then should you quarrel and dissolve the partnership you will each be entit-led to half the value of the lawn-mower. If, on the other hand, you have had a busy summer and, after paying all your expen-ses, you have £200 in the partnership's bank account, then the taxman will treat your 50 per cent share of that as personal income, even though you have not drawn a penny of it. The snag is that if your neighbour takes you to court over the unfortunate affair of the prize dahlias and gets awarded £500 in damages then, if your best friend can't or won't fork out his £250 share, £500 worth of your wife's jewellery may still be in danger—even if it was in fact your partner who did the damage. Worse still, if your partner doesn't pay the tax due on his share of the partner-ship's profits you could find yourself liable for that, too.

A further point about a partnership is that participation or 'shares' in it cannot be transferred. This is particularly import-ant when it comes to matters of inheritance. A father, for exam-ple, cannot leave a share in a partnership to his child: what he can leave is the value of his share; on his death the partnership is then dissolved automatically and, if the other partners are will-ing, it can be reformed with the heir as a new partner.

Though a partnership can be held, in law, to exist even when there is no formal agreement between the partners it will nor-mally be governed by a deed of partnership, drawn up by a soli-citor and signed by all the partners. Clearly, such a document is essential. It will lay down the rules of the partnership, provide for what should happen in the event of dissolution or the death of a partner, etc. It can also provide for one or more of the part-ners to be a 'sleeping partner', that is, to participate by provid-ing finance and drawing a share of the profits but not to take part in the work of the partnership; or, to take another example, for one of the partners to receive no share of the profits though retaining his original stake. One important point to look out for is that the deed of partnership should clearly state what individ-ual partners may or may not do in the name of the partner-ship—what debts they may incur, what agreements they may sign, etc—without the consent of the other partners. If your partner in Arcadia Landscape Services is as reckless with a pen as with a mower, then it is as well to make sure that he cannot sign an agreement to landscape the local park and a cheque for a new bulldozer without your consent. In the absence of a deed to regulate such matters you could find yourself with a very busy summer and a whacking debt to the bulldozer dealer.

A limited liability company

The third way of organising a business is as a limited liability company. Since it is unlikely that any part-time business will attain the size and complexity which makes its incorporation desirable, and because anyone who does reach this stage will certainly be well-advised to go into it more thoroughly than space in this book allows, we will deal with this third possibility more sketchily. The basic points about a company are that it has a legal existence totally separate from its owners and employees, and that its liability is limited to the net value of its assets. If, for example, your lawn-mowing business has so grown and flourished that it has transformed itself into Arcadia Landscape Services Ltd and has made a profit of £50,000, then the company will have to pay corporation tax on that amount, but you, as an employee and shareholder, will only be taxed on the sums you have drawn by way of salary or paid yourself as a dividend. On the other hand, unless there is some special provision in the company's Articles of Association, there is nothing to stop your fellow shareholder selling his shares in the business to your deadly enemies, The New Brutality Concrete and Paving Co, leaving you in a very awkward situation. But if he has continued to cut a swathe through valuable flora, and the company has a grass-box full of writs from furious gardeners, or simply has no customers left and has to go into liquidation, then you can take comfort from the fact that your only loss will be the amount of money you invested in the business; the creditors have no claim to your personal property.

The structure and formation of companies, and the law governing them, are complicated; no one should consider setting up a company without proper professional advice from a solicitor and an accountant, which does not mean that you do not need to understand the issues. The saying, 'garbage in=garbage out', coined by the computer business, applies just as well to professional advice. Unless you give your advisers all the facts, ask the right questions and make sure that you understand the answers, then the fees you pay are wasted—remember they are *advisers*, not decision-makers.

Raising money

Whatever formal status your business adopts, its first requirement is, very likely, going to be a bank account and some cash to put into it. It is almost certainly worth opening a separate bank account for even the smallest business. The bank statement is a basic piece of documentation and you only complicate life if you have to check constantly to see whether a debit of some item represents a new pair of shoes or a vital piece of equipment for your workshop. Your bank manager will be happy, if you explain the situation, to set up a separate account, even if it's only the 'Bill Smith No 2 account'. In certain circumstances you can even make arrangements for monies to be transferred automatically from business to personal accounts and vice versa. For example, it could be wasteful, if you are a sole trader, to be paying interest on an overdraft of £100 in your business account while you have £1000 sitting idle in your personal one.

Unless you have personal savings to put into the business, finding something to put in the account will be a bit more difficult than opening it. For small businesses seeking start-up funds (that is, cash to buy the equipment and stock which most new businesses require in order to get going), the source will probably be a local branch of one of the big high street clearing banks. Other sources of capital, apart from family or friends, are almost certainly not going to be interested in a part-time enterprise—their organisation and procedures are geared to larger ventures, and bigger amounts of money.

Dealing with your bank
In practice you are almost certainly limited to the bank and branch which you use for your personal account. This is because the two things which any bank manager is going to want to be sure of are that your project is viable (a point we will come to in a moment) and that he has security for the loan or overdraft facility which he is going to provide. He will naturally feel happier and safer if he has had your personal business in the past and is going to keep it in the future; moreover, he may want you to deposit securities in the form of stocks and shares, or even a mortgage on your house, and this is much more easily arranged if all your banking business is under one roof. But remember that the big banks do compete with each other, and if you feel that your present manager is being unreasonable or unhelpful there is nothing to stop you investigating the attitude of his rival across the street—though that will probably mean transferring all your business to your new bank. In the case of a partnership where the individual partners bank at different

49

branches or banks you have a choice and can, perhaps, introduce a bit of healthy competition between your respective managers, but when you settle on one bank for the partnership's account remember that the manager may well want a good deal of information about the affairs of the partner who banks elsewhere, reasonably so if he is being asked to provide substantial sums of money.

However much you may think of your bank manager as a friend, even a helpful friend, when you ask him to lend money for your business you are asking him to make a business decision—that decision will certainly be influenced by his assessment of your personal qualities, but he would rather lend £10,000 to his worst enemy who can offer a sure-fire proposition and sound security than £1000 to his best friend who couldn't run a jumble sale and is flat broke.

The key facts to bear in mind when dealing with bank managers are: first, they are there to lend money, that's their business; so when you ask yours for help you are offering him a business opportunity in just the same way as you offer business to a garage when you go to buy a new car. Second, before the bank manager lends money, he has to be sure that the venture you are proposing has a reasonable chance of success and that if, for any reason, it fails, he can be certain of recovering his money.

So, unless you are already in deep financial water or have a bad financial track record, you can start from the assumption that your bank will want to help, and that it is up to you to show that you have a sound idea and the skills necessary to implement it. No bank manager will be impressed if he has to drag the information he needs out of you, finds that you have overlooked essential factors or have not gone to the trouble of presenting your case as clearly and professionally as possible. On the other hand, he will be immediately impressed by evidence that you have worked the thing out thoroughly, considered all the snags, and provided him with an easily understandable proposition. So it is well worth investing time and trouble in preparing the best possible presentation. You can then put this to the bank. At some point your manager is certainly going to want to discuss it with you in person, but he will probably want a chance to study your proposition and your figures first, so the best approach is probably to write, enclosing all the information you wish to present, and explain that you will be happy to call and discuss the project with him when he has had time to consider it.

To convince him that your proposition is a good one you have to provide clear information on the following basic points:

- Exactly what you plan to do
- Your qualifications for undertaking the work
- The amount of money you require and what it will be used for
- Any evidence you can offer of the market for your goods or services
- Financial forecasts (cash flows and, perhaps, profit and loss accounts) for at least the first 12 months showing that your enterprise will generate sufficient profits to pay the interest on the debt and, ultimately, to repay the principal.

It is essential to strike the right balance between too little information and too much, especially in dealing with the first point. For example, 'I plan to bake cakes' is brief to the point of uselessness, but 'I plan to bake devil's food cakes using the recipe from *The Sarah Lee Cookbook* and sell them for 50p each to that nice Mr Donizetti at the Il Piazzetta Delicatessen and Patisserie, 23 Gas Works Road...' is burdening the bank manager with far more detail than he needs. In all but very exceptional cases the presentation should take up no more than three or four typewritten pages, plus a page or two of figures. The kind of figures and the methods of preparing them are dealt with below (see page 68).

Security

The question of security can be dealt with in your covering letter, or left for discussion at an interview. But you should prepare yourself by listing, at least in your head, the various sources of security which you can offer. If you are seeking money to buy equipment then that in itself may offer some security. But though that new bandsaw may be just what you need for your joinery, and cheap at £750, it may be worth a good deal less to the bank, especially when it has had a few months' use and is bolted down to your workshop floor. The commonest security of all is, of course, your house. A bank manager will almost certainly have a working knowledge of property values in his area, so a formal valuation is unlikely to be required, but he will need details of your mortgage(s) as this reduces the proportion of the house's value available to the bank as security; if the title deeds are not already held by a building society, he may ask you to deposit them with the bank, or even suggest a legal mortgage in the bank's favour. Other possible forms of security include stocks or bonds, valuables in exceptional cases, or a bank guarantee. In the last case, your borrowing is guaranteed by someone, a member of your family or a friend, who can satisfy the bank that, in the last resort, they will be in a position to make good any loss the bank suffers if you default on your debts. Often a friend or relation who knows and trusts you well enough to offer such help may prefer to give a guarantee of this kind rather than lending you the money directly, which might involve, for instance, selling securities or realising assets which he or she would prefer to hang on to. The golden rule, when it comes to giving security, is to be a pessimist. Do not gaily sign away your house on the assumption that all will go well, and even if it doesn't, that nice bank manager will never evict you. Things may go wrong and, in the last resort, banks are not kind-hearted institutions.

Overdraft or loan

Assuming you clear all these hurdles and your bank makes a firm offer of help, it will be in one of two forms. The commonest, and in most cases the most appropriate for a part-time business, is a straightforward overdraft facility—that is an agreement that you may overdraw on the account up to a set limit. Banks charge interest on an overdraft at an agreed number of percentage points above their 'base rate'. For the kind of business we are discussing the figure they will have in mind is 2 to 3 per cent 'above base'. Base rates, of course, now vary, according to government policy and economic conditions, and there is limited competition between the big banks in keeping their base rates down. Any alterations will figure prominently in the financial pages of the national press, so you should not have any difficulty in keeping in touch with your own bank's current base rate. Remember that the number of points over base which you pay is negotiable and if you are a large or favoured customer you may persuade your manager to reduce the rate he charges you. It is also worth bearing in mind that banks do not necessarily charge interest to all customers on the standard quarterly basis; again, if your manager has a particular reason to be nice to you he may agree to charge on a six-monthly basis, a real saving since for half the year you are not paying 'interest on interest' which you would be doing on a quarterly basis.

The alternative to an overdraft is a term loan. This is a loan of a lump sum, at an agreed, fixed rate of interest for a set period, anything from three to ten years in most cases. The loan will usually be repayable in instalments at set dates, commencing anything from a few months to two years from the starting date.

The advantages of a loan, as opposed to an overdraft, are that you know how much interest you will be paying, it will not fluctuate with the bank's base rate, and that once made it cannot be revoked until the due dates—an overdraft is, in theory at least, recoverable at any point the bank chooses. In practice banks do not recall overdrafts unless things are looking very bleak indeed, though they may well press you to reduce your limit when they make their annual review if they feel that your business is not justifying the present limit or not doing as well as you forecast.

The disadvantage of a loan is that you may find yourself borrowing money, and paying interest on it, when you really do not need any or all of it. If your business is likely to be one where the cash situation fluctuates violently over short periods, resulting in a bank account that swings from the red to the black and back again, then you will be better off with an overdraft, paying only for borrowing when and to the extent that you actually need it. If, on the other hand, it is one that requires a large fixed investment at the outset, which will be repaid over a long period at a regular and predictable rate, then a loan may be preferable.

Other sources
Before leaving the subject of borrowing, it is worth mentioning one alternative to your bank which is open to you if you have a life insurance policy. It is not very widely known that insurance companies can and do lend money to beneficiaries against the accumulated value of life policies. Obviously, if you have only recently taken out the policy and have made only a few monthly payments, then the policy will have little value, but if you have been paying in regularly for 10 or 15 years or more then this may be a very useful source of money for a part-time business. The insurers will charge the current commercial rate of interest on the loan and you must remember that, if you die or the policy matures before you repay the loan, then the amount paid out by

the insurer will be reduced by the amount of the loan plus any accumulated, unpaid interest. You can establish the current loan value of your policy quite simply by writing to the insurance company and asking them, but remember to quote the policy number if you do so.

If you are fortunate enough to be able to borrow direct from family or friends you must insist that there is a formal document covering the terms and conditions of the loan—rates of interest, repayment dates, etc. However confident you are that Aunt Edith can spare the money and intends to leave it to you anyway, a sudden death or an unexpected row can find you dealing with executors or lawyers who care not a whit that you were always a favourite nephew or that Angela Moneybags was your best friend at St Theresa's 20 years ago.

Employing an accountant

Whatever the size or form your business takes, you will have to produce accounts. A company is, of course, obliged by law not only to produce annual accounts and to lodge a copy at Companies House, but also to have them audited by a chartered accountant who can certify that they give an accurate picture of the company's affairs. A partnership also has, by law, to produce accounts, though unlike a company's, these do not have to be audited and are not public documents. A sole trader will be well advised to produce accounts if he does not want to see his profits vanish down the maw of the Inland Revenue. Any business, however competent the person running it, will probably need the services of an accountant at least to get its annual accounts into final form. In the case of a partnership or sole trader, the accountant employed does not have to be fully professionally qualified—many professional bookkeepers or audit clerks are more than capable of the work involved—but should you need advice rather than more or less mechanical accounting skills, then you should insist on getting it from a fully qualified professional. Both bookkeeping and accountancy are, by the way, fields in which many spare-time earners are active (see Chapter 6), so it may well be sensible to give the modest amount of work your business requires to an individual rather than to a firm of accountants.

The nature and the amount of help you require from an accountant will vary enormously according to the nature of your business, and the extent to which you are able and willing to deal with basic bookkeeping chores yourself. But it will almost certainly be worth taking professional advice right at the outset on the following:

- Any agreement dealing with loans or financial support other than a straightforward overdraft facility at your bank
- The extent, timing and methods by which you withdraw your second income from the business
- A partnership deed
- The formation of a limited company
- The basic bookkeeping requirements of your business.

Failure to get advice on any of these points could cost you time, trouble and efficiency or, most likely of all, additional tax. It is important that you choose an accountant whom you can get on well with; not only can he or she be an invaluable source of business advice, but, as we shall see in the next chapter, will almost certainly be taking care of your personal financial tax affairs. You should also remember that not all accountants are equally good at everything; Mr X may be just the man to advise you if you want to set up a family trust in the Netherlands Antilles for tax purposes, but you should no more dream of consulting him about your part-time business than you would take your ingrown toenail to an open-heart surgeon.

Basic records and bookkeeping

Any business is going to involve paperwork and this brings with it two possible dangers. If you are the kind of person who hates and despises the stuff, then you will have to overcome your revulsion; on the other hand, if you are the type who compulsively files everything from school reports to butchers' bills, then you are going to have to tame your magpie instincts. You do need to be able to lay your hands quickly, for example, on the invoices you issued last month and you will not be able to do so if they are 'somewhere' in a two-foot thick wodge of miscellaneous paper, nor if your filing system is of a sophistication more appropriate to a multinational corporation. Common sense and experience will soon produce solutions which suit your own particular line of work. A system of recording receipts which suits a spare-time decorator, doing perhaps a dozen jobs a year,

RECEIPTS

July 1989	Cheques	Cash
18 Hendersons Ltd (32 hours + £4.60 postage)	£132.60	
August 1989		
3 Kogan Page Ltd (6 hours)	£24.00	
27 A J Smith (20 hours)		£80.00
September 1989		
10 Sue Grabbit & Runne (14 hours legal typing @ £5/hour)	£70.00	
28 Super Designs Ltd (16 hours plus £5 for extra carbons)		£69.00
Totals for 3rd Quarter	£226.60	£149.00

PAYMENTS

July 1989	Cheques	Cash
3 High Street Stationers		£5.60
Acme Office Supplies (ribbons and carbons)		£3.44
10 Postage		£4.60
August 1989		
1 Paddy's Paper Ltd (paper) Cheque no 887614	£15.00	
15 To personal account Cheque no 887615	£150.00	
September 1989		
9 Paddy's Paper Ltd (paper) Cheque no 887616	£12.80	
30 Acme Office Supplies (typewriter service)		£10.00
Total for 3rd Quarter	£177.80	£23.64

RECEIPTS

June 1989	Invoice No	Catering	Retail	VAT	Total
10 Hon Margery Ffolkes	6/01	£254.00		£38.10	£292.10
12 Dolly's Dell (May account)	5/06		£93.00		£93.00
16 High St Bakery (April account)	4/02		£165.24		£165.24
24 County Ladies Guild	6/02	£100.30		£15.04	£115.34
Total for June		£354.30	£258.24	£53.14	£665.69

PAYMENTS

June 1989	Cheque	Materials	Equipment	Motor Expenses	VAT	Total
1 Bricks Catering Supplies (Inv 0641A)	61403	£160.00				£160.00
6 Evans Electric (new oven)	61494		£400.00		£60.00	£460.00
21 Station Rd Garage (petrol)	61495			£8.00	£1.20	£9.20
28 Plonk Wine Co (wine)	61496	£67.90			£10.18	£78.08
Bricks Catering Supplies (Inv 175/M)	61497	£101.24			£5.00	£106.24
		£329.14	£400.00	£8.00	£76.38	£813.52

will be totally inadequate for a playgroup organiser who has to collect weekly payments from 15 absent-minded parents; on the other hand, the decorator may be purchasing hundreds of pounds' worth of materials from different suppliers, whereas the playgroup may require no more than a couple of expeditions a year to top up its equipment, so their systems of recording outgoings will, again, vary.

There will be few spare-time businesses whose filing should occupy more than a couple of drawers in a filing cabinet. But do discipline yourself to get everything filed weekly or monthly; do keep copies of your own letters, orders and invoices and receipts or vouchers for cash disbursements. Don't leave that valuable order or the bank statement lying about where they are likely to become part of your children's *papier mâché* model.

For most part-time enterprises a room, however small, which can be set aside for 'business' use is a near necessity, but even if you have to make do with a corner of the living room or a desk in your bedroom, do clearly establish the fact with your family or flatmates that this space, desk or table is sacrosanct and not available for use as a sideboard.

The cash book
Even if the documentation for your month's work is as simple as, say, receipts for the purchase of a ream of typing paper, a packet of carbons and two typewriter ribbons plus an invoice to your customer for 32 hours' typing at £4 an hour and £2.60 postage, you will still save yourself trouble, and your accountant time, if you keep simple books recording your transactions. At its simplest, your book-keeping system will be a simple cash book. A cash book records money (not just cash, but cheques and other monetary instruments) going in and coming out: when it was received or paid; who from or to; and the item, invoice or goods to which it relates. It can be as simple as an ordinary school exercise book or one of the many easily available accounts ledgers with the left-hand side of each opening used to record receipts and the right payments, as set out in the example on page 56.

The totals (weekly, monthly or quarterly according to the particular business) are an essential aid to keeping track of your 'cash position' (an accountant's expression which means no more than the amount of money in your bank or at hand, or your current borrowings) and for checking your bank statements. In the example on page 56, of course, if you had simply pocketed the cash payments you received rather than paying them into your business account, you would have to record them as personal withdrawals on the right-hand page as well as receipts on the left if your record of your business cash position is to remain accurate. Note that separate columns are kept for cash transactions on both sides.

If your business is at all complicated, or there are particular kinds of expenditure or income upon which you wish to keep a check, then it may be sensible to break one or both sides down into categories. If, for example, you are charging a part of your motoring expenses to business use, then it will be convenient to have a separate column for these, and if you are registered for VAT (see page 98), it is crucial to keep the VAT element separate for all entries. It is also important to separate purchases of equipment, etc from raw materials or stationery and office supplies; or suppose you are regularly supplying delicatessen items to shops and catering for parties, then having a separate column for each kind of business in the cash book will clearly be appropriate. If your record is analysed in this fashion then you will, at regular intervals 'cast and cross cast' the totals—the result will look something like the table on page 57.

Note that in the case of payments you should, where appropriate, always record the suppliers' invoice number or other reference and in cases where you are paying by cheque you should record the cheque number which will help you to reconcile your own records with your bank statement. You should make a point of doing this every time you receive a statement, not only because banks are fallible, but also because it will act as a check on your own accuracy. Before attempting a reconciliation you will, of course, have to add to the right hand side of the cash book any charges or interest which the bank has debited to the account in the period. If you still do not agree with the bank, then make sure that one of your own cheques is not still outstanding (ie has not been presented for payment by the recipient). Your reconciliation will look something like this:

Balance at 30 April		£346.24 od
Outgoings for period per cash book		£249.68
Cash in hand		£5.00
		£600.92
LESS		
Income for period per cash book	£367.90	
Cheque outstanding (No 88896785 V Tardy & Co)	£27.00	
	£394.90	
Balance at 30 June		£206.02 od

If your final figure agrees with the bank's, then all is well; if not, one or other of you has made an error, and you will have to start checking the items against the statement, your cheque book counterfoils and paying-in book.

Cash transactions

If your business involves a lot of cash transactions, or many small payments made in cash, then you must be sure to keep a very accurate record of these as well — your accountant and your tax inspector will not be satisfied with a vague recollection that you must have spent the £41 which is unaccounted for on postage, travel or 410 feet of two-by-one. So if, for example, a customer gives you a bundle of 20 fivers for redecorating his living room (assuming that it is not your intention to cheat the taxman, a subject we will come to in the next chapter) and you spend £24 of it on wallpaper for another job, £30 on a new step ladder and £15.95 buying drinks for your mates in the pub, then you may well find yourself the following morning with a bad hangover and a challenging accountancy problem — unless, that is, you gave your customer a receipt for £100 and kept a copy of it together with the receipts from your builders' merchant, in which case you know that you should enter £100 on the receipts side of the cash book and on the payments side, £24 in the column for materials, £30 under equipment, £15.95 under personal drawings and that you have, somewhere about your person, £30.05 which you can pay into the bank, add to the cash in hand or to the item for personal drawings.

The best answer to this kind of situation is to carry with you a small notebook in which you jot down the details of such transactions. If the shop where you buy your materials does not issue proper receipts, but only those little rectangles of paper that look exactly like bus tickets, then do, at the first opportunity, make a list of the items purchased and their individual cost and staple it to the slip from the cash register. If you have spent money on items such as fares or stamps for which you have no documentation, then make out a petty cash voucher for yourself with details of the expenditure and the date.

You can deal with petty cash in one of two ways, either by keeping a float on hand, in which case life will be easier if you keep it separate from your personal money, or by paying such expenses out of your own pocket and then reclaiming them from the business. You may say that if you are a sole trader the distinction is meaningless, all the money is yours anyway. The answer to that is twofold: first, as we will see in the next chapter, the price of not keeping such records can be a much higher tax bill than necessary; and second, if the overhead expenses of your business are simply lumped together with everyday living costs, you have no chance at all of working out on what basis you should price your goods, charge for your services, how much profit you are making, or even if you are making one at all.

Daybooks and ledgers
A cash book is a record of receipts and payments as and when they actually occur. What it does not keep track of is sums owed and owing, essential information in all but the simplest businesses. The need is easily met for most part-time businesses by some simple system, such as keeping unpaid bills and your own invoices which await payment in a couple of bulldog clips and filing them away only when payment has been made or received and entered into the cash book. But if a great many small sums are involved, or if the business is a complex one from the accounting point of view, it may be worth keeping daybooks and ledgers for sales and/or purchases. A daybook simply records, in date order, invoices raised or received by the business (for some unfathomable reason, invoices are not made out, despatched or issued but 'raised') with details of the account and the sum involved; like the cash book entries, these can of course be analysed under different headings and if you are registered for VAT it is vital to isolate the VAT component since this

tax is payable or recoverable not on payment of an invoice but on the date of the invoice (see page 100). Each entry can be marked off as you receive or make the payment concerned.

The entries from your sales and purchases daybooks are 'posted' to the sales ledger and the bought ledger and these provide a means of keeping track of what is owed to you, or by you to other people. The left hand page of each opening in the ledger contains, in the case of the sales ledger, details of the invoices you have raised; in the case of the bought ledger, of invoices you have received. In each case the entries are made in date order with the same details as in a daybook. The right hand page contains, in the sales ledger, a record of receipts (ie it will match the left hand page of the cash book as far as credit sales are concerned); in the bought ledger it records payments made against the bills detailed on the facing page (thus it will match those items on the right hand page of the cash book when you have received credit rather than paying on the nail).

By totalling both sides of your ledgers at regular intervals and deducting the running total of the left hand page from that of the right hand one you can calculate, from the sales ledger, how much you are owed by customers and, from the bought ledger, how much you owe to suppliers. As we shall see shortly, this can be information that is crucial to running your business, and will certainly be something that your accountant has to calculate even if you do not; for your profit or loss for the year is not measured by the balance on your bank statement plus the cash in your pocket, but by balancing what you owe (including any borrowing from the bank) against what you are owed (including the money the bank owes you if your account is in the black).

If your record keeping goes beyond the simple cash book stage, you should certainly get your accountant's advice on the kind of books you need to keep and the form they should take. You will probably also need to understand the basic elements of bookkeeping; many books are available which explain the subject in lay language, and one I would recommend as being particularly clear and up to date is *Practical Guide to Good Bookkeeping and Business Systems* by John Kellock (Business Books, 1982).

Controlling credit

The granting and receiving of credit (ie the delay between the date of an invoice and its payment) is one of the critical factors in any business. This becomes obvious when you look at it as a matter of borrowing or lending. If you deliver goods to a customer and he takes three months to pay his bill then either you are unable to buy the new materials you had earmarked that money for, or the grocery bill you were going to withdraw it for, or, more likely perhaps, you withdraw the money from the bank anyway and have to pay interest on it for the whole quarter. Conversely, if you can stave off a creditor you are, in effect, borrowing money from him for free which you might otherwise have had to borrow from the bank and pay interest on. The aim, therefore, must always be to collect what is due to you as fast as possible and pay what is owed by you as slowly as possible.

As a small business you have advantages and disadvantages in this often ruthless game. When it comes to collecting what is owed to you, you must accept that, in the case of large companies, you come pretty low on their list of priorities; on the other hand, you may have more time and energy to badger, bully and beg than a bigger creditor can spare. In other cases, you have a better argument for asking for prompt payment or cash on the nail than some vast company whose computer has thousands of accounts to keep tabs on. When it comes to taking credit, your account is not likely to be of a size that will call for more than routine reminders for some time when it comes to bills from large organisations—small local tradesmen are obviously a different matter. The one factor that moderates give and take is the need to maintain goodwill: it is absolutely pointless to delay paying your supplier for six months if, as a result, he decides not to do business with you, to demand cash on delivery or, worst of all, you end up on some credit blacklist within your trade. In the same way, you will not keep or increase your customers if you turn up on their doorstep 24 hours after sending an invoice with a couple of strong-arm men behind you. It is also worth remembering that, particularly at a time when interest rates are high, the granting of a discount may be a substitute for credit—if you have regular suppliers, especially small or medium-sized ones who know you personally, then ask about the possibility of receiving a discount for prompt or immediate settlement. As you can easily calculate, when a supplier is paying 16 per cent per annum for a bank overdraft it will be worth his while to give you a 2½ per cent discount for cash if the alternative is waiting two months for his money. If you have spare cash sitting in a current account earning no interest it will be worth your while too; but if the positions are reversed then perhaps it is you who should be seeking credit and offering your customers a discount for prompt payment.

Invoicing

The bit of paper fundamental to this whole process is the invoice. There is nothing complicated or mysterious about it; at its simplest it is any sheet of paper, headed 'Invoice', dated, clearly marked as being 'from' your name and address 'to' the name and address of your customer and setting out the details of the goods or services supplied, the amount due for them and the credit terms, (see example on page 65).

A variation on the invoice theme is the 'pro-forma' invoice. A pro-forma is used where no credit is to be given. Suppose, for example, the unfortunate Mr Mortice has learnt from bitter experience that Space Age Toys pay at a very stone age speed. He may insist on dealing with them on a pro-forma basis: if they send him an order, then he will send them an invoice requesting them to return it with payment in full before he delivers the goods. Pro-formas are used most frequently, for obvious reasons, when individual customers order relatively cheap items through the post: to deal with them on a credit basis would be both costly and risky.

If your business is going to involve raising a great many invoices then it may be worth getting forms or pads specially designed and printed; if not, you can simply use your letter-headed paper. The one vital thing to remember is to keep a copy, not only because it is your record of the transaction but because your customer is fully entitled to ask for a copy if he loses or 'cannot find' the original. If the transaction concerned is a one-off sale, then the simplest way of chasing up payment is to send a copy of the invoice, perhaps accompanied by a letter reminding the customer that payment is due, or in cases of persistent 'bad payers' threatening legal action, etc. But if you are dealing with a customer on a regular basis then you may be expected to send him a monthly statement. This should have three columns of figures: the left hand one, Debits, showing amounts invoiced since the last statement, with details of invoice number, date etc; the centre one, Credits, showing payments received since the last statement; and the right hand one showing, at the top,

---

INVOICE

30 June 1989

To: From:

Messrs Space Age Toys   James Mortice
24 The Mall   'Chippings'
Smallbridge   The Common
Dorset DT14 1JL   Chortleton
                             Dorset DT14 8PB

---

20 wooden galactic rockets
at £1.20 each   £24.00
(your order No 456/B)

Terms: 30 days net

---

the Balance brought forward (ie the amount owing on the previous statement) and at the foot the Balance now due.

The needs and methods of a business when it comes to invoicing and granting credit will vary enormously. If you are doing building or substantial decorating work, for instance, you will almost certainly have agreed an estimate with the customer (see page 84) and you are entitled to ask for progress payments to cover the costs of time and materials as you go along, so your final invoice will have to relate to the estimate, give details of any additional items subsequently agreed with the customer and take account of monies already received by way of progress payments.

But if you are selling goods by mail order then you will, as we have seen in the previous chapter, probably be asking for payment in advance, either by inviting customers to send the money in with the completed coupon or by sending them a proforma invoice. In that case you will send a receipt with the goods, and your record of the sale will be your copy of the receipt, which should contain details of the goods and sums involved, as on an invoice, plus words such as 'received with thanks' and the date.

Many private individuals will pay on receipt of your invoice, but business customers may, as we have seen, expect credit. You must state what this is on your invoice usually in the form

'Terms: 30 days net' (the net simply means that no discount can be taken). 30 days is the commonest credit period, but if longer credit is to be given it is usually calculated in multiples of 30: 60, 90 or 120. Most business customers will, however, interpret 30 days as meaning 30 days from the end of the month in which the invoice is dated; thus they will expect to pay an invoice dated 1 April at the end of May. The man who looks at a pile of invoicing work on 31 March and decides to go to the pub and leave it until the morning will truly be an April fool.

The point of all this paperwork is twofold: first, you have a record of what you sold, to whom, when and for how much, which you can match up with your cash book and your bank statements if the taxman queries anything; second, you have a record of the credit you have given, to whom and for how long. Keeping the credit you give to the minimum, 'controlling' it as business jargon puts it, is, as we have seen, essential. Copy invoices, an up-to-date cash book and, where appropriate, a sales daybook or ledger are the tools of credit control, the ways in which you use them will depend on your business, your customers and your character, but at least you will know when you ought to be going into action and on which fronts.

STATEMENT OF ACCOUNT

May 1989		Debit	Credit	Balance
Brought forward from April statement				£26.08
Invoice 012	May 18	£16.00		
Cash	May 20		£25.08	
Invoice 132	May 29	£23.45		
Balance Due				£40.45

Stock

Allowing too much credit is one way of wasting money by having it tied up unproductively in materials which you have bought or work which you have done but have not yet been paid for. The other one is stock: raw materials, partly finished goods (work in progress) or completed but unsold goods. In an ideal business the raw materials required are delivered at the back door just as you require them and the finished goods go out of the front door into the customers' hands with the paint still tacky—and, indeed, people like motor manufacturers go to great lengths to get as near as possible to this blissful state of affairs. But most of us have no choice, stock is a necessary evil if we are not to spend our lives buying materials in penny packets and keeping our customers waiting. If you are manufacturing anything, on however small a scale, stock is money sitting idle— money which you are paying for the use of. Say you are a cabinet maker. That lot of exquisite rosewood may have looked like a bargain when the merchant offered you a 10 per cent discount to clear it; but if half of it is still sitting in your storeroom two years later you have probably had the worst of the bargain. Suppose the full price was £500 and you paid £450 after allowing for the discount. The merchant has taken your £450 and turned it over several times in the interim, making a profit each time, you on the other hand have probably paid your bank some £75 to £100 in interest for the privilege of admiring the grain, and your business may have suffered from the shortage of cash as well.

The speed with which you turn over your stock—that is, purchase materials, turn them into finished goods, sell them and collect the money to buy more materials—is known as your rate of 'stock turn' and is a measure of your efficiency. For example, a business which starts the year with £100 and turns it over ten times, making a profit of £20 each time, is making twice as much profit as the one which turns the same £100 over only two and a half times, even if the latter is making twice the profit on each turn. Moreover, the latter is, in effect, raising its prices to make up for its inefficiency, and will certainly succumb in any competition between the two.

This is, of course, an area in which different kinds of business are not comparable, any more than a supermarket which reckons, probably, to turn its stock over once a fortnight can compare with a stockholding bookshop which may be lucky to achieve an annual stock turn of two. What the spare-time business can do, however, is to check constantly that it is not holding unnecessary stock and that the true cost over time of every purchase is carefully calculated.

67

Annual accounts

When your accountant prepares your annual accounts—and, by the way, your business's financial year does not have to end with the calendar year on 31 December or with the government's financial year on 5 April; there may well be advantages in choosing a different date and you should ask your accountant's advice on this—he will be summarising your business performance. In the case of a company there are three separate documents: the trading account, the profit and loss account and the balance sheet. Though the accounts of a sole trader or a partnership may be much simpler than those of a company, the same principles apply and it is worthwhile making sure you understand them thoroughly even if your own formal accounts are limited to a summary at the end of your tax return.

The trading account

The trading account calculates the gross profit—that is, the difference between the price you paid for your goods—in most cases material and labour—and the price you obtained for them. In the left-hand column you will see your inputs, that is, the cost of the materials and labour you have purchased during the year (whether or not you have actually paid for them), *plus* the value of the stock which you had at the beginning of the year and *less* the value of the stock you have at the end of the year. On the right-hand side are your outputs, that is, the value of your sales (again, it is irrelevant whether you have been paid for them or not). The difference between the two is the gross profit or gross loss. But a gross loss would be a remarkable achievement even for the least successful because, as we shall see, gross profit is a very long way from net, or real profit.

But, if your business is one which involves holding substantial stocks, you should be aware that your gross profit figure can conceal something much nearer to a gross loss than you would like. The key is in the figures for stock. Normally, stock is valued at cost, what you paid for the materials, plus the value of labour involved in the case of work in progress or finished goods. All well and good, if you are going to need those materials and can sell those goods at full price. But put yourself, briefly, in the position of Mrs Thorndike and Mrs McIver, the partners in Trendy Tops of Twickenham. Fourteen months ago the two

Miranda Dresses—Trading Account for 1989

	£	£
Sales		6578
Purchases	2550	
Opening stock	763	
	3313	
Less closing stock	657	
		2656
Gross profit		3922

ladies struck it rich: they had designed a lovely silk blouse with
mother-of-pearl buttons and started producing it just as silk
blouses became all the rage; they couldn't make them fast
enough and recruited friends and neighbours to help. Every
sewing machine between Kew and Wimbledon was going ham-
mer and tongs. Alas, just as quickly as they had come 'in', silk
blouses with mother-of-pearl buttons went 'out' and denim
waistcoats with brass buttons came 'in'. Mesdames Thorndike
and McIver are now ruefully contemplating three gross of
blouses which are about as saleable in the Kings Road as Bibles
in Tehran. Even if they could find a customer, they would be
lucky to get a price which covered the cost of the silk, let alone
the £3 a blouse which they paid to the seamstresses of south-
west London. As their accountant will tell them, that stock has
to be written down in value, if not written off completely. To
leave it in the trading account would not only be fooling themselves, it will also mean that the Thorndike and McIver families
will be paying a lot more tax than they need to. The more the
profit, the more the taxman is going to take, and there is no
point in leaving those blouses in the accounts at cost, when the
loss on them is a perfectly genuine one and by writing them
down at least some tax can be saved. If, by any chance, this policy proves over-pessimistic and the blouses can be sold for a
good price, then the amount written off, or a proportion of it,
will have to be 'written back' the next year.

The profit and loss account

To arrive at your net profit, the amount of money you have really made, your accountant produces a profit and loss account. This starts with your gross profit and deducts from it all the other expenses of running the business—travel, telephone, heat and light, entertainment and rates, his own fees, etc and interest which you have had to pay to the bank. If your business is a company, or a partnership where you draw a salary in addition to a share of profits, he will also deduct your salary, but in the case of a straightforward partnership or a sole trader your earnings and your profit amount, as we have seen, to the same thing. What is left is your net profit (pre-tax profit in the case of a company).

Miranda Dresses—Profit and Loss Account for 1989

	£	£
Gross Profit		3922
Less: Expenses		
Telephone	143	
Travel	254	
Entertainment	123	
Rates	289	
Heat & Light	261	
Bank interest	376	
Postage	154	
		1600
Net Profit		2322

There are a few complications. The calculations that are produced for the taxman will differ from those that you need for your own purposes. This is because there are items such as entertainment of guests which, while a perfectly proper business expense, are not allowable for tax; your taxable profit will therefore, alas, almost certainly be greater than your net profit in the profit and loss account. But more of these tax matters in the next chapter.

The balance sheet

The third product of your accountant's labours, certainly in the case of a company or partnership, will be a balance sheet. Unlike the other two accounts, this is not a record of what you have done during the year, but a statement of where you stand at the end of it. Balance sheets can be confusing things, if only because there are many different ways of arranging them, but the end result is always the same: to show what the net worth of the business is and how, supposing it was closed at that moment, its value would be divided up to leave a neat, tidy and empty kitty. Obviously, the net worth and the value available for distribution have to balance exactly, hence the title.

The simplest form of balance sheet simply shows the assets, ie property, stock and debtors of the business on the right-hand side, and its liabilities, ie what it owes to others, on the left-hand side. At first glance it might seem odd that one should always balance the other, but it makes sense when you realise that the difference between the two is made up of any money the owners have invested in it and any profit which it has made; these two items are both liabilities because they are owed by the business to its owners. In the case of a company there may be 'retained' profits or 'accumulated' losses from previous years which are brought forward and which add to (or, in the case of losses, reduce) the company's liability to its shareholders. In the case of a partnership the profit for each year will be distributed among the partners, at least on paper.

Most company balance sheets will in fact be organised rather differently, to show on the right-hand side the net value of the company, ie its assets less its liabilities but not, in this case, the money it owes to its shareholders in the form of capital invested and accumulated profits and reserves (reserves are usually retained profits that have been set aside for a particular purpose or to cover contingencies). These items, the shareholders' funds, make up the other, left-hand, side of the balance sheet. Often the two parts are set out one above the other, the 'right-hand' side, the sum of the business' assets coming first, followed by the details of the owners' funds headed: 'represented by' or 'financed by'.

Miranda Dresses—Balance Sheet as at 31 December 1989

Fixed assets	£	£	£
Plant & machinery	3256		
Less depreciation	814		
			2442
Current assets			
Stock	657		
Debtors	2100		
Cash in hand	5		
		2762	
Less current liabilities			
Creditors	364		
Bank overdraft	250		
		614	
			2148
			4590
Represented by			
Capital			2268
Profit for year			2322
			4590

When you look at a balance sheet in this form it becomes clear why it is not strictly necessary to draw one up for a sole trader; since the business is part and parcel of the individual's possessions, the left-hand side of a balance sheet for his business would simply be a single figure, the value of the business as set out on the left-hand side. Moreover, it is of no interest to anyone except the sole trader and the tax inspector if he chooses to add the cost of the family holiday to the business's liabilities or to include the washing machine in its assets.

In the case of a partnership or a company, the left-hand, or lower part of the balance sheet shows how the value of the business is divided between its owners. In a partnership's balance sheet, it will be divided into two categories: the partners' capital accounts and their current accounts. If, for example, Miranda Dresses was a partnership between Mrs Mirren and Mrs Anderson, to which each had contributed £1000 when they started out, and if each had drawn £750 during the year, then the bottom part of the balance sheet might look like this:

Capital accounts		£	£
Mirren		1000	
Anderson		1000	
			2000

Current Accounts	*Mirren*	*Anderson*	
	£	£	
At 1 January	957	811	
Share of profits	1161	1161	
	2118	1972	
Less drawings	750	750	
	1368	1222	
			2590
			4590

Thus, of the total value of the business—£4596—Mrs Mirren is entitled, at this point, to £2374 and Mrs Anderson to £2222.

In the case of a company, where profits can be retained without being apportioned to the shareholders, the situation would be slightly different. If Miranda Dresses was a limited company, with Mesdames Mirren and Anderson each owning 1000 shares of £1, the bottom part of the balance sheet might look like the table on page 74. Note, however, that their drawings of £1500 would have been deducted as an expense in the profit and loss account, so their net profit is now £822.

It can be seen that the accumulated profit brought forward from previous years is the equivalent of the opening amounts in the partners' current accounts and that the new total of accumulated profit carried forward is the equivalent of the partners' current accounts at the end of the year. If, as in the case of the partnership, the proportion due to each shareholder was not the same, then this would be the result of money they owed the company, or were owed by it, which would be included under 'Debtors' or 'Creditors' in the top half of the balance sheet.

Ordinary Shares (2000 shares of £1 each)		2000
Accumulated profits brought forward	1768	
Profit for year	822	
Accumulated profit carried forward	2590	2590
		4590

However the balance sheet is arranged, the most significant ingredients are usually the Assets and Liabilities. Assets are divided into two: fixed and current. Fixed assets are property and equipment such as tools, motor vehicles etc, which the business needs to do its work. Though such things are not bought and sold by the business but, once purchased, kept for use, they do diminish in value, or depreciate. Just as Trendy Tops' blouses had to be written down in value, their sewing machines and delivery van must be depreciated if the accounts are to show their real value. The way in which a business deals with depreciation is largely determined by tax considerations and so is dealt with in the next chapter, but the point to note here is that it will show up either as a cost in the profit and loss account or as a deduction from the value of the fixed assets in the balance sheet.

Current assets are stock, debtors (ie the money owed to the business) and cash. Liabilities are not usually divided into current and fixed. Normally they will consist of creditors (money owed by the business) and its overdraft or short-term borrowing. If there are long-term loans, then they will probably show up on the left-hand side with a note of the date at which repayment is due.

Obviously, the total value of assets less total liabilities equals the theoretical value of the business if you decided to sell it lock, stock, and barrel at the date on the balance sheet—its 'break up' value. Equally obviously, this is almost certainly not a reflection of what you would actually receive.

If you were forced to sell the business, stock, equipment and all, piecemeal, then you would be likely to get very much less than you would expect to receive if those items were sold over a period of time in the normal way, a balance sheet therefore is really expressing the value of the business as a 'going concern'.

On the other hand, if you do sell, let us say, your prosperous cookery enterprise, Quality Quiches, to the giant Universal Pie combine then you will expect them to pay you a lot more than the balance sheet, or asset, value. This is because you are selling not just your ovens, delivery van and stocks of flour, eggs and bacon, plus the money owed to you and less the money you owe, but also the reputation you have built up, your excellent contacts with shops and the potential profit to be made from these intangible assets. If Universal Pie does come across with a handsome cheque, then the difference between the price they pay and the balance sheet value of the business will be labelled 'good-will'. Accountants and business men are suspicious of good-will appearing in a balance sheet and usually try to write its value off as quickly as they can, for very good reasons. Suppose that Universal Pie decided that Quality Quiches would be even more profitable if, instead of butter and fresh eggs, they were to use margarine and powdered eggs. The good-will you took ten years to create might be, literally, eaten away in weeks.

Analysing your accounts

The crucial items in most accounts will be these: in the trading account the sales, or turnover, for the year, and the 'cost of sales' (that is, the difference between the sales and the gross profit). If sales do not increase, then in a period of inflation, the business is obviously shrinking. If the cost of sales, as a percentage of sales, goes up, then one of three things is happening: you are spending too much on materials or labour, you are not charging enough for your goods, or you are making more than you can sell. If the last is the problem, then either your stock will be increasing out of proportion to your sales or you are writing off unsaleable stock. Dividing the figure for closing stock into the sales total will give you your rate of stock turn (see page 67).

The profit and loss account is basically an analysis of your overheads. The items to watch here will obviously vary from business to business, and you will be able to spot the ones you need to keep an eye on, but 'bank interest' is one that will be common to many.

The balance sheet can be analysed in a number of standard ways. The ratio between current assets and current liabilities, the 'current ratio', shows how 'liquid' the business is, ie how easily the income from sales will cover its short-term debts. But stock may, of course, not really be a 'current' asset if it is going to take a long time to sell it, so deducting the stock item from current assets and dividing what is left (in most cases simply debtors) by liabilities (in most cases simply creditors plus overdraft) makes the so-called 'acid test'. Finally, the net worth of the business, the figure at the bottom of both sides of the balance sheet, is also the 'capital employed', ie the amount of money the owners have invested in the business. If you divide this figure by the annual profit, then you get a percentage which is your 'return on capital'.

This last is a crucial figure. If, for instance, you are thinking of borrowing money in order to expand then you should check that your return on capital is higher than the rate of interest you will have to pay; if not, and if the business earns the same return in the future as it has in the past, then not only are your interest payments going to eat up the extra profit you hope for, they are also going to reduce the profit you are already making. In the same way, if your return on capital is lower than the rate of interest offered by the Post Office or a building society you would be better off with a nest egg than a business.

Forecasting and cash flow

All the figures we have dealt with so far are records of what has happened—very useful and important, especially when you have been going for several years and can compare your present performance with previous years, both overall and for individual items. But even more important is what is going to happen in the future. The business version of the crystal ball is the cash flow forecast, and this is what, for example, your bank manager will want to see when you put your initial proposition to him. But the forecast is more than just a tiresome test set by bank managers; for every business it is the equivalent of a budget for the year, a plan which must, as the year goes on, be checked against reality. For your cash flow is just as crucial a test of the health of your business as its profit. Look, for example, at Fred Filigree and Charlie Ming, spare-time antique dealers. Their accounts show a handsome profit, for three months ago Fred bought a collection of Georgian silver for £1000; last week Charlie sold half of it to Mrs Pinchpenny for £900 and he knows that an American client will pay just as handsomely for the other half when he makes his annual visit in a couple of months' time. So Filigree and Ming's trading account looks like this:

	£	£
Sales		900
Opening stock	—	
Purchases	1000	
Closing Stock	500	
Gross Profit		400

They had invested £100 in the business which has been spent on overheads, so their net profit is £300; the balance sheet looks like this:

Partners' capital accounts	100	Fixed assets	
		Current Assets	
		Stock	500
		Debtors	900
			1400
Profit for year	300	Liabilities	
		Creditors	1000
	400		400

But this cheery picture vanishes if the auctioneer from whom they bought the silver is about to send the bailiffs in and Mrs Pinchpenny notoriously refuses to settle any account for six months. Filigree and Ming may have a nice profit but their cash flow is a disaster. To avoid this sort of problem, and the infinitely more complicated versions of it which even a spare-time business can encounter, a careful cash flow forecast is essential.

Deirdre Glaze, the potter, is pretty good at this sort of thing, so let's see how she goes about it. She produces a range of earthenware pots and dishes which she sells to local shops who, in turn, sell them to tourists during the summer. Though Deirdre has to keep up a steady rate of work all through the year to produce enough goods, the shops aren't interested in stocking up with them until May at the earliest. They pay her bills at about 30 days on average, and by the end of September the last tourists have left. The position is complicated by the fact that

Deirdre needs a new kiln. She has a small stock of clay and other materials but will soon need more. She gets 30 days credit from suppliers and she has an electricity bill for £60 which she will have to settle in January. Alas, her business account has only £150 left in it—she drew most of last year's profits and blew them on a wild weekend in London looking at Greek vases in the British Museum with her friend Patrick Patina.

Deirdre's outgoings are going to look something like this:

	J	F	M	A	M	J	J	A	S	O	N	D
Purchase of kiln		720										
Materials		50		75			75			75		50
Electricity	60			60			60			60		
Misc overheads	8	8	8	8	8	8	8	8	8	8	8	8
Total	68	778	8	143	8	8	143	8	8	143	8	58

She is clearly going to need an overdraft in the first part of the year but will only know how much and for how long when she has worked out her income, which goes like this:

	J	F	M	A	M	J	J	A	S	O	N	D
Sales						950	950	950	950	950		

Deducting one total from the other, and starting with the £150 in her account, she calculates her monthly cash position, and she can then see what she is going to have to borrow from the bank.

	J	F	M	A	M	J	J	A	S	O	N	D
Cash position												
Income						950	950	950	950	950		
Outgoings	68	778	8	143	8	8	143	8	8	143	8	58
Cash (overdraft) B/F	150	82	(696)	(704)	(847)	(855)	87	894	1836	2778	3585	3577
Cash Position Before Interest	82	(696)	(704)	(847)	(855)	87	894	1836	2778	3585	3577	3519

If she assumes that her bank's base rate is going to stick at the current 13 per cent and she has to pay 2½ per cent above base, it is going to cost her just under 1.3 per cent per month, but the bank will actually debit her account in March and June, so she adds the interest for the first quarter to her outgoings for March and that for the second to June. If she plans to draw on the business for personal expenses, then she must of course allow for this in her outgoings. It looks as if she will have to have a frugal spring, but she should be able to afford another fling with Mr Patina in the autumn!

Being the efficient young lady she is, Deirdre will check the actual figures for each month against her forecast as well as taking account of changes of circumstance. If, for example, the Electricity Board suddenly raises its prices by 20 per cent, then she has got to revise her whole forecast. The costing of her produce is going to be totally different and she is going to have to see whether she can economise somewhere, charge more for her goods, manage a combination of the two, or just accept a lower profit.

Cash flow forecasting obviously gets easier when you have been running the business for a reasonable period, as you have past costs and sales to go on, and you know the items that have to be looked at with especial care. But remember, making a forecast of cash flow is even less reliable than making a forecast of the weather; just because you say it is going to happen doesn't mean it will. So always veer on the side of caution and allow for the unexpected. You and your bank manager will be delighted if you do better than your forecast, but all the hindsight in the world won't help your bank balance if you do worse.

Producing that first, vital forecast for the bank manager and for yourself at the outset is naturally much more of a shot in the dark. But it has to be done, even if it is your own savings, not the bank's money, you are investing. You will surely want to work out on paper exactly how soon you can expect to get the money back. You will have to do a good deal of investigation, finding out what the equipment you need will cost; how much credit your customers are going to expect; what advertising or selling costs you should allow for; how much the household's bills are going to increase by and, of course, how much you can charge for your produce. If what you *should* charge is more than what you *can*, in terms of the current market, charge, then you do not need to go on to forecast your cash flow—the equation will not work out. Costing is the other essential bit of crystal ball gazing that you have to do, and we are coming to it shortly. But first, in case you are asked for, or want to make in any case, a forecast of your profit and loss account and even your balance sheet, then it is easy once you have done the cash flow.

All you have to do is remove the element of credit at the beginning and add it on at the end. If, at the beginning of the year, you owe X and are owed Y, that comes into your *cash flow* because you will have to pay out X and hope to receive Y in January, but X and Y have already gone into last year's *accounts* so will have no place in this year's. If at the end of the year, you reckon you will owe A and be owed B then the two figures are irrelevant for the cash flow but must go into the forecast of profit and loss, and into the forecast balance sheet as liabilities and assets. Money spent on fixed assets (capital expenditure) does not come into the profit and loss account but does have to go into the balance sheet, after allowing for depreciation.

Costing and estimating

Costing

As well as being a forecaster of almost preternatural skill, Deirdre Glaze has also mastered the art of costing. This is not only a matter of working out what it costs to make your goods, and therefore what you should charge for them; it may also be a question of whether you should make this or that item at all, whether it is better to make a few and sell them at a high price or mass produce them and sell them cheaply, etc. Deirdre tackles costing this way.

Her starting point is that her costs divide into two categories: fixed and variable. Her fixed costs are her equipment, for the sake of simplicity that new kiln, which she has to pay for whatever she does, and things like telephone, stationery and postage which she lumps together as miscellaneous overheads. She also treats delivery costs as fixed since it costs as much to deliver one vase in the back of her Mini as a gross of ashtrays. The variable costs are her materials, the electricity to fire her pots and her own labour. What is a fixed cost and what a variable will vary. The principle to remember is that fixed costs are items which you are going to have to pay anyway—purchase of equipment, insurance, general overheads, heat and light, rent and rates, are standard items—whereas variable costs are those which relate directly to the goods you are making or the service you are supplying—raw materials and labour being the obvious ones.

In Deirdre's case her fixed costs for miscellaneous overheads and delivery, averaged out over the year, come to £8 per month. She has also worked out with her accountant that she should depreciate her kiln over three years, writing off a third of its value each year, so the depreciation cost per month is £20, giving her a total of £28 per month. (She need not, of course, use the same rate of depreciation in her costing as her accountant advises for tax and accounts purposes. She can try to recover the cost more quickly, raising the price of her pots, or spread it out over a longer period if necessary.) Deirdre is trying to decide whether to spend her spare time in January and February making some of the rather elaborately decorated garden urns, which she tried out last year, or whether she would be better off turning out the mugs which bore her stiff but always sell. One urn uses, she calculates, 5p worth of clay and 30p worth of glaze. Each takes her an entire evening, say four hours, to make, and her kiln will only fire two of them at a time, consuming 50p worth of electricity in the process. Deirdre also reckons that she needs to make at least £4 per hour for her spare-time work.

Assuming she works five evenings a week, or 20 days a month, producing 20 urns, costs for a month's urn-making are:

Fixed Costs	
—Depreciation	£20
—Overheads	£8
Variable Costs	
—Materials	£23
—Electricity	£10
—Labour	£320
	£381

Dividing this equally between the 20 urns, she gets a 'unit cost' of £19.05. If she can sell the urns for £20 apiece then she is making a profit, even after 'paying herself' £4 an hour.

On the other hand, she can turn out mugs by the dozen while giving half her mind to *Coronation Street* on the TV. Let's say that she can manage 20 an evening, and that they only cost 3p apiece in materials and, since she can cram them into her kiln, only 2p apiece in electricity.

The cost of a month's production of mugs, 400 in all, is therefore as follows:

Fixed Costs	
—Depreciation	£20
—Overheads	£8

Variable Costs

— Materials	£12
— Electricity	£8
— Labour	£320
	£368

The unit cost of the mugs is therefore 92p. In fact, Deirdre sells them at £1 each, so her profit on a month's worth of mugs is 400 x 8p, or £24, whereas on the urns it is 20 x 95p, or £19. She will be better off making mugs. But suppose she knows that the five shops that tried out the urns last year will certainly ask for more; indeed, they admired them so much that they would probably pay her £25 each provided they are not pressed to buy more than two each. In that case she will calculate that it is well worth while having a rest from the mug production line for a fortnight, losing £12 profit, but instead turning out just ten urns which will, at £25 each, give her a handsome profit of £5.95 each or £59.50.

A full-time business, employing labour, would certainly do its costing this way. But the question for a spare-time business may be rather different. You, after all, do not have to work at all, so if you prefer it you can cost the work out omitting the charge for your own time, and combine the labour charge and the profit into a single figure.

There was, in fact, another option open to Deirdre. Though the local shops could sell only a small number of her expensive urns, she had recently seen an advertisement in a gardening magazine offering what was clearly an inferior kind of urn at £35 apiece. She had discovered the magazine's circulation and its advertising rates and had also made inquiries about the cost of packing her urns and having them delivered by rail. What would happen if she placed a half page advertisement and invited the urn-loving public to buy her superior urns at £35 each, including delivery? Well, a half page would cost £110 and Mr Patina, who is a good designer as well as a potter, was prepared to design a tasteful advertisement for £10. The cost of packing and delivering an urn came to £3.60. The question was, how many urns did Deirdre have to sell to show a profit?

The unit cost of the urns was, we recollect, £19.05. The difference between that and the selling price of £35 is £14.95 from which she has to deduct packing and carriage costs for each urn sold of £3.60, leaving a margin of £12.35, out of which she has to pay for the advertisement which cost, with the design, £120. A quick sum shows her that if she can sell ten urns she will be making a profit, that is her 'break even' figure, but of course on every urn she sells over and above that figure she will be making a generous £12.35.

Deirdre was so encouraged by this, and so confident that people would respond to her advertisement, that she wondered if she couldn't do even better. If she simplified her design a bit and worked an extra hour a day she could double her rate of urn production, but on the other hand she would have to charge a bit less, say £30, for the simpler model. She decided to cost out the alternatives.

One month's urn production	Model A	Model B
Fixed Costs		
— Depreciation	£ 20	£ 20
— Overheads	£ 8	£ 8
— Advertisement and Design	£120	£120
Variable Costs		
— Materials	£ 23	£ 46
— Electricity	£ 10	£ 20
— Labour	£320	£400
Total	£501	£614
Unit Cost	(div 20) £ 25.05	(div 40) £ 15.35
Receipts per urn	£ 31.40	£ 26.40
	(£35 − 3.60 p&p)	(£30 − 3.60 p&p)
Margin per unit	£ 6.35	£ 11.05

So far so good. Obviously, the simpler urn is the better proposition, as it will produce a profit of 40 x £11.05 or £442 for a month's work, whereas the original design will produce only 20 x £6.35 or £127. But, and it is an important but, Deirdre then worked out the break-even figure by dividing the total costs of each month's work by the amount she received for each urn. Thus for Model A the break-even point comes at £501 ÷ 31.40 or, in round figures, 16 sales; for Model B, on the other hand, it comes at 614 ÷ 26.4, or 24 sales. If she sold 16 Model As Deirdre would at least have covered her costs, including her own labour; but if she sold only 16 Model Bs she would have lost £191.60, or nearly half the value of her month's labour. Urn A was a safe proposition, whereas Urn B was a gamble which might fail but

which would, if it came off, pay for Deirdre and Patrick Patina
to take a package trip to Athens.

Estimates

An estimate is really just a costing which you show to the customer and agree to stick to under certain conditions. This time
you start with your variable costs: how long it is going to take
and what materials it is going to use. You will have a pretty
good idea of your fixed costs per week, month or quarter, and
you have to add to the variable costs of materials and your own
labour a fair portion of those fixed costs. You will, also, if you
are prudent, add something for contingencies. Remember, your
client will be delighted if your final bill is a few pounds less than
the estimate, even if he thought the estimate a bit stiff in the
first place. On the other hand, he will be dissatisfied if you
tender a very low estimate and then add on a host of trivial
extras to the bill.

An estimate should always be agreed in writing, and it should
be clearly stated that it is subject to current prices for materials, etc. If, of course, a genuine additional and unforeseeable
expense turns up in the course of the job, you are perfectly
entitled to charge for the additional work involved. But you
should notify the client in writing of what the additional cost
will be and get his agreement to it.

The golden rule is never to underestimate the fixed and overhead costs. Building that linen cupboard for Mrs Proudy across
the road is not just a matter of 30 feet of two-by-two softwood,
some battening and plywood and four or five hours' work. You
are going to have to collect the timber in the van, consuming
petrol and time, you will be using that super new power saw for
which you just paid £60, and don't forget that you have just
spent nearly an hour measuring the job up and doing the
estimate!

4. You and the Taxman

It would be idle to deny that, for many people, one of the strongest attractions of a spare-time income is the hope that it will also be a tax-free income. We have all read about the 'black economy' and seen those well-dressed chaps in Jaguars who have such a noticeable aversion to cheques. Why not join in? In the end the decision is for each individual's conscience; all this book can do is point out some of the snags.

Look, to start with, at the cautionary, and true, tale of Ms Lindi St Clair. She ran a business in West London, more full-time than spare-time, it seems, which provided 'personal services', largely of a 'disciplinary' kind, to lonely but well-heeled gentlemen. This enterprise prospered so greatly that she decided to turn it into a limited company; but this plan ran into an obstacle in the shape of the Registrar of Companies who, when Ms St Clair applied, refused to sully his Register with terms like 'hooker' or even 'French teacher'. Outraged at such narrow-mindedness, Ms St Clair decided to drag the Registrar, kicking and screaming if need be, into the permissive society. She took him to court and, after a well publicised hearing, lost. Bad enough. But the reports of the case caught the ever-watchful eyes of the Inspectors of Inland Revenue who concluded that, for a business lady contemplating incorporation and able to afford a High Court action, Ms St Clair was overly modest about her success when it came to filling in her tax returns. They visited her premises, in a purely professional capacity, inspected her 'dungeon' and other capital assets and in due course delivered *their* form of discipline—an assessment of tax liability for over £10,000.

The tale of Lindi St Clair has two morals for the tax dodger. One, if you are going to avoid tax you will have to avoid publicity as well. Those watchful eyes that scanned the law reports could just as easily fall upon your advertisement or a story about your spare-time work. Two, if you do get caught, all those records you carefully didn't keep become a liability rather than an asset. In the absence of proper evidence about the extent of your profits, the taxman's guess is as good as yours—but he can make his stick.

The tax dodger also has to try and run a business in which the true level of sales and profits has to be concealed. He has constantly to bear in mind which bill from a supplier has to be kept and which invoice to a customer has to be 'lost', and how the connection between the two can be disguised. He cannot discuss his affairs frankly with a bank manager or an accountant; he cannot give a written estimate or take a slow payer to court; he doesn't like taking cheques or giving receipts; and if he ever needs capital to expand then he cannot show evidence of his past success to a bank or an investor. Anyone who has quick enough wits, a good enough memory, and sufficient guile to prosper under handicaps like that would probably do even better in a *bona fide*, tax-paying business.

For the purpose of this book we will, therefore, assume that you do not combine the acumen of John D Rockefeller with the duplicity of Kim Philby—probably the minimum qualifications for successful tax dodging—and that you intend to play it straight with the Inland Revenue. None of which means, of course, that you intend to pay a penny more than you have to.

The first thing to consider is what you will have to pay tax on, and what can reduce the bill; we will then go on to look at how the tax on your part-time income affects or is affected by the other taxes you pay or benefits you receive, and when and how you pay. If you are embarking on earning a spare-time income for the first time, you should note that it is legally incumbent upon you to tell the taxman of your new source of income within 12 months of the end of the tax year (5 April) in which it began. It is no excuse to say that no one asked you or sent you a tax return to complete.

Taxable profit

Sole traders and partnerships
The profit, for tax purposes, of a sole trader or a partnership, is all the income that flows into the business, less what the Inland Revenue call 'allowable expenses'. To keep track of what comes

in is pretty simple: you just have to make sure that the £20 you won on the Derby doesn't stray into the accounts. Allowable expenses are a bit more complicated: basically, they are all the costs involved in your business: materials, goods for resale, wages, overheads, etc. The exceptions and points to note are as follows:

1. Providing your business involves the use of your home as a workplace or office, a proportion of household bills such as electricity, rent, rates, gas, telephone, insurance, etc is allowable. You should, however, be aware that if you take advantage of this you may run into trouble if and when you come to sell your house. Normally, provided it is your 'sole residence', any profit you make on selling a house is not subject to Capital Gains Tax. But if you have been claiming household expenses against business profits, then the Inland Revenue may argue that some proportion of the profit from your house represents the sale of a business asset rather than a residence and tax you accordingly. (See below under 'Capital Gains and Inheritance Tax', page 93.)

2. Annual depreciation of your fixed assets—car, tools, equipment, etc—is not deducted from profit as an allowable expense, but is instead dealt with by a system of 'capital allowances' which achieves the same effect. You can depreciate most items at the rate of 25 per cent per year (this does not mean that the whole amount is written off in four years; in year one you write off 25 per cent of the purchase price, but in year two 25 per cent of the remaining 75 per cent).

3. Though it may seem unlikely that any spare-time business will be paying wages, it will, as we shall see, be very much in the interests of the family budget as well as marital harmony if a married man pays a wage to his wife. Note that if a partner draws a salary from the partnership in addition to a share of profits, then that is not an allowable expense.

4. Interest is allowable, provided it relates to borrowing for business purposes: if you go into overdraft when you book the family holiday on the Costa Brava you may have a job persuading the tax inspector that you made any number of useful business contacts on the beach and

that your bank interest is therefore allowable. Keeping a separate business bank account, as suggested in Chapter 3, will greatly simplify this item. If a partner lends money to a partnership and charges interest on the loan, that interest is not, however, allowable, so it may be better for the partnership to borrow from the bank than from you. (It won't in the end affect your partner's tax bills, but it will increase yours.)

5. If you have purchased equipment on hire purchase, then the capital repayments qualify for capital allowances and the interest is an allowable expense.
6. If you have a bad debt which you can identify and show is unlikely to be recovered, this is allowable.
7. Travel and motoring expenses are allowable, but if they seem large for the size of your business, the taxman may ask you to explain exactly what painting and decorating services you were performing, for example, in St Moritz during April. Entertaining is not an allowable expense.
8. If you are not registered for VAT (see Chapter 5) then the VAT on allowable expenses is itself allowable, but if you are registered you will already have recovered it and, of course, the VAT which you charge on your sales is not part of your taxable income.

What remains of the business's income after the deduction of allowable expenses and capital allowances is its taxable profit. In the case of a sole trader, this is added to other income for the purposes of computing the income tax payable. In the case of a partnership, the profit is divided between the partners in the agreed proportions, and if one or more partners receives a salary or interest on a loan to the partnership, then that will count as a part of that partner's share of the profits. Each partner is then assessed for income tax on the basis of his total income—ie his share of the partnership's profit plus income from other sources—but the share of his tax bill which relates to income from the partnership is payable by the partnership, not the individual partner. This means, as we saw in the previous chapter, that if one partner dies or becomes insolvent, the others could be liable for the tax on his share of profits.

Companies
Most spare-time businesses will operate on a sole trader or

partnership basis. There are few advantages for a small-scale business to gain from becoming a limited company; as far as taxation is concerned, the change of status can even be a positive disadvantage, because losses incurred by the business cannot be offset against tax paid on income from other sources, and because directors are treated as employees of the business and taxed on a PAYE basis. The main difference between a company and a sole trader or partnership, as far as tax is concerned, is that instead of the individuals involved paying income tax on the profits, the company itself pays corporation tax. Though the full rate is 35 per cent, this is only reached by companies with a turnover of three-quarters of a million pounds. Small businesses (with profits of less than £150,000 per year) only pay 25 per cent.

National Insurance

If you earn a spare-time income you will almost certainly be liable to pay National Insurance (NI) contributions in various forms or permutations. The rates change from year to year, so do check the current position—leaflets are available from local social security offices.

Reforms of National Insurance introduced in the 1989 Budget will take effect from October 1989, and will help to mitigate the NI burden for those on lower incomes.

First, if you work for an employer, you and your employer pay Class 1 National Insurance contributions, unless you earn less than the NI threshold of £43 a week, in which case you pay nothing. Once you earn more than £43 a week, you will pay employee's contributions of 2 per cent on the first £43 and 9 per cent on earnings of between £43 and £325 a week. No NI contributions are payable on earnings above £325 a week.

If your spare-time income is from self-employment then, regardless of whether or not you have a full-time job and pay Class 1 contributions, you may have to pay Class 2, and perhaps Class 4, contributions as well. You do, however, escape them altogether if you are a man aged over 65 or a woman aged over 60, or if your spare-time income is less than £2350 a year—in the last instance, though, you have to apply for exemption and should ask your social security office for the relevant leaflet. Class 4 contributions are, in effect, a levy on profits from self-employment between £5050 and £16,900 per year at the rate of

6.3 per cent. They are collected by the Inland Revenue, along with income tax.

Income tax

How and when you pay

We have seen that the income left after deduction of allowable items from your spare-time work, if you are a sole trader, is added to the rest of your income in order to arrive at the total upon which you are assessed for income tax. The most significant concession to be taken advantage of in the case of a married man will usually be the wife's earned income allowance; provided that you can show that she is actively helping you with your work, you can 'pay' your wife up to £2785 per year (at current rates), and save income tax on that amount. You simply show this sum as an allowable expense in your accounts and provided that she has no other source of earned income your wife does not owe tax on it.

If you pay income tax under Schedule E (ie if your employer deducts PAYE from your paypacket), you will receive a tax return every year shortly after 5 April. To see how you, or your accountant, deals with this let us take the case of Harvey Feinlein. Harvey works as a graphic designer in an advertising agency, and a couple of years ago he started to earn some income from freelance work in his spare time. Previously, completing his tax return had been a matter of ensuring that he included details of his children, mortgage, and life insurance policy to get the allowances he was entitled to; the only income he had was from his employers, and their PAYE returns told the tax man all about that.

Now he has to turn his attention to the section headed 'Trade, Profession or Vocation'. Here he will enter the total income he received from his freelance work, say £6000. He will also give a total of allowable expenses (or 'balancing charges') and capital allowances which he is claiming. Say he spent £400 on stationery and other materials, purchased a new drawing board for £600 and spent £300 on travelling to see clients, etc. He also decides that the help his wife gave him was worth every penny of £2785. Harvey's allowable expenses are £400 (materials), £300 (travelling) and £2785 (wages) and he claims a capital allowance of £150 (25 per cent of £600) on the drawing board. He also has to remember to enter £2785 against the question on wife's earnings in the 'Employment or Offices' section of the form. Provided that the taxman has no queries, he will assess Harvey for income tax on a spare-time income of £6000 less £3635, or £2365.

If Harvey does nothing else, the taxman will simply adjust his PAYE code so that he pays the tax due over the course of the next year in PAYE contributions. But, if Harvey sees no reason to show his employer that he is earning a spare-time income, or if he simply does not want to pay his additional tax in monthly instalments, he can apply to pay it direct, in which case his bill for the past year will be payable in two instalments, one on 1 June and one on 1 January.

Harvey may also decide that he wants to close his accounting year not, like the taxman, on 5 April but on, say, 31 December. In this case the figures he gives will cover the 12 months ending on that date. In fact, being smart, Harvey sees that if he ends his financial year on 30 April, it will be nearly 11 months before he has to declare his profit. In the meantime he will be paying tax on a preceding year basis — ie based on the profit he made the year before, which, even if he is doing no better than keeping in step with inflation, will be lower than this year's.

In order to get the new business's taxation on to this 'preceding year' basis, the taxman does some complicated juggling. Suppose Harvey started up his freelance work in June 1987 and ended his first financial year on 30 April 1988. He would not totally escape the taxman for a whole year until 6 April 1989; instead he would have to tell the inspector, on his 1987-88 return, that the profits were 'to be agreed' and when he had done his accounts he would report what that profit was. During the year beginning 6 April 1988, he would pay tax on the profit he made up to 5 April, or an agreed proportion of his total profit; during the year beginning 6 April 1989 he would pay tax based on the profit he made up to 30 April 1988, ie mostly the same profit as he was taxed on before. Only during the tax year beginning 6 April 1990, when he would be paying tax on his profits for the year ended 30 April 1989, would Harvey be established on the preceding year basis.

This is fine if Harvey's business is growing each year — he has achieved his object of delaying the tax bill on his profit as long as possible. But if his first few months of business were very successful and after that it was downhill all the way for Harvey, then during 1989 and 1990 he will have been paying tax on profits he was not, in fact, making. To avoid this, Harvey can apply to be taxed in the second and third year of his business on the basis of the actual profits he made rather than on the profits of the preceding years.

If things go really badly for Harvey and he actually makes a loss, then he can set that off against other income—his salary, for example—and reduce his tax liability.

In the case of partnerships, partners will not necessarily pay the same amount of tax—their liability will depend on individual circumstances (eg whether married or single, whether they have income from other employment, etc).

The preceding year arrangements work in exactly the same way for partnerships as for sole traders. If one partner uses his car or house for business purposes then he may claim a proportion of his motoring or household expenses as an allowable expense against his share of profits. If the partnership owns the car, then you will have to negotiate with the tax inspector over the extent to which you use it for private purposes, and how much of this use should be taxed as a benefit.

If a sole trader or partnership ceases trading, then the preceding year system has to be unravelled. If, for example, a business closes down in the tax year ended 5 April 1989, it will have, at that date, paid its tax bill for 1987-88 on profits made in 1986-87, and would normally pay in 1989 on the basis of profit for 1987-88; it will therefore have to settle up for the amount by which profits in 1987-89 actually exceeded those for 1986-88. Because, as we saw in Chapter 3, a partnership is in theory dissolved and reformed if there is a change of partners, it is assumed by the taxman to have ceased trading and started again unless within two years of the change he is formally notified that it is continuing.

The taxation position of limited companies is more complicated; if your spare-time activity develops sufficiently for it to be worthwhile changing to limited company status, then seek advice from your accountant on how this affects the way in which your business is taxed.

Making the most of your tax allowances

With his or her spare-time income, as in most other tax affairs, the single person has no real room for manoeuvre. Apart from claiming any allowances for mortgage interest, pension contributions, dependants, etc to which they are entitled, there is little the unmarried can do except pay up.

The married man can take advantage, as we have seen, of his wife's earned income allowance. If he is a sole trader, he can pay her the maximum of £2785; if he is a member of a partnership he can, with his accountant's advice, so arrange matters that she receives the same amount either as an employee or as a partner herself; and if he has formed a company then he can, again, pay her that sum as a salary. In each case, of course, this assumes that the wife really is helping with the business. Where it is the wife who is earning the spare-time income, things are not so easy. She will, of course, escape tax on the first £2785 of her profits, but after that her income will be added to her husband's for tax purposes so there is no advantage in paying him for his help.

The only other possibility is for husband and wife to elect to be taxed separately. This only becomes advantageous if both are very high earners, for the immediate consequence of separate taxation is that the husband ceases to be entitled to the married man's allowance and the wife loses her wife's earned income allowance, though she gains the basic personal allowance. The equation will not work out to your advantage unless your combined incomes push you into the higher tax bracket (income tax currently rises from the basic 25 per cent after you have earned £20,700 of taxable income and is payable at 40 per cent above this figure). If you are making the sort of money that brings this solution into the realms of the possible, then you should set a little of it aside to pay for your accountant's advice on the subject.

Pensioners and claimants

In general, a spare-time income will not affect your entitlement to pensions and benefits—except of course in cases like Family Credit which is only payable when income falls short of a certain level, or unemployment benefit where entitlement depends upon your being available for work if it is offered.

Capital Gains and Inheritance Tax

If your spare-time income involves you in building up a business or acquiring substantial assets in the form of equipment, etc, you should be aware of those twin terrors, CGT and IHT

(Inheritance Tax). The spare-time enterprise to which these posed a real problem would probably be an exceptionally successful one, or one which had burgeoned into something more like a full-time business; nonetheless, if your venture involves equipment the cost of which runs into thousands rather than hundreds of pounds they could come as a nasty surprise to you or your heirs.

CGT is a tax on the profit you make, in cash or on paper, when you sell an asset. If, for example, you have bought an elaborate lathe for £1600, had it for three years, in each of which you claimed the 25 per cent capital allowance, or a total of £925 (25 per cent of £1600 + 25 per cent of £1200 + 25 per cent of £900), then its 'book value' is now £675. If you then sell it for £1000 you have made a capital gain of £375. Provided you keep your total capital gains in each year below the current threshold of £5000 you are safe, but it can be seen that this can pose a threat if you have built up a substantial stock of equipment over the years and then decide to give up your work and sell it off. As mentioned earlier, you can also fall foul of CGT if you have been claiming a proportion of your household expenses as allowable business expenses, for some part of your house has then become a business asset in the eyes of the Inland Revenue. However, no CGT is payable if a room or rooms are only *partly* used for business, even if you have claimed some of the running costs of the house as expenses. CGT is assessed only on the part of the house used solely for business. Additionally, if you reach the age of 60 and have been running your business for ten years, you qualify for CGT relief on the first £125,000 of gains, and half of your gains between £125,000 and £500,000 when you sell your business assets.

If you choose not to sell your business assets but to give them, or leave them in your will, to someone other than your wife or husband, then IHT looms. IHT is levied at a single rate of 40 per cent on assets of more than £110,000. However, this will scarcely be likely to affect the assets of a spare-time business, except when combined with other assets. Your lathe is not a problem, unless you have turned it to such good effect that you have become the owner of a villa in the Bahamas or a pile of Krugerrands, in which case it makes a small contribution to the large bill for IHT which your executors will have to face up to.

The best advice for the spare-time business, where CGT or

IHT is concerned, is to consult your accountant if you think that any steps you are contemplating may attract either tax—accountants always use the curious term 'attract', for all the world as if you took your capital gain down to the offices of the Inland Revenue and fluttered your eyelashes at the inspector!

5. Miscellaneous – But Important

The law

Even if you earn your spare-time income entirely on your own, without partners, let alone as a limited company, you are, in the eyes of the law, a sole trader as explained in Chapter 3. You are therefore subject to the whole battery of statutes which regulates trading in Britain. For example, if you sell a pot of jam, labelled as containing 1lb net, which contains only 15 ounces you are, in the eyes of the law, just as much an offender as the giant manufacturer who sells 100,000 underweight jars.

Where a particular line of work is likely to involve legal implications the fact is mentioned in Part II, but certain general rules apply. You must describe your goods honestly and accurately; you will be liable for damages if goods supplied by you turn out to be dangerous or damaging to the health of consumers; if you employ anyone, even on a casual basis, to work in your home, you are subject to the Factories Act so that if, for example, the half-witted lout you hired to help out over the weekend manages to injure himself on your lathe, you could be in serious trouble.

On the other hand, of course, there are instances where the law can be on your side. You are, for instance, quite entitled to take non-paying customers to court—provided you have kept proper records and can establish the existence of the debt.

The most likely area of conflict is with local authorities. This may not arise out of officiousness on their part, but as a result of complaints from neighbours or others. For example, if you regularly use your house as a workplace or place of business then, technically, you should apply to your planning authority for a 'change of use' from residential to industrial or commercial. In practice, it is unlikely that anyone will bother you unless your activities reach a scale, or a nuisance level, at which they become conspicuous or objectionable. An exception will, however, arise if your spare-time work necessitates alterations to your property, or additions such as a workshop, which require planning permission. In that case you will certainly have to put your cards on the table. Provided that what you are doing does not affect the character of the district or disturb your neighbours, there should be no real problem. You may, however, find that the local authority will want to rate the property as commercial, instead of on the lower residential scale.

The Environmental Health Department of your council will be concerned if your work involves the preparation of food or the use or storage of noxious or dangerous materials, or if you are involved in breeding or boarding animals (see page 159).

It is unlikely that your activities will attract the attention of the police, but if you start causing obstructions or traffic hazards—by, for example, setting up a roadside stall, attracting customers who cause a parking problem or taking cars apart in the street—you may find that you are in breach of a surprising number of regulations.

Your house

If you do not own the freehold of your house, but rent it or own a lease, you should check the lease carefully. It may well contain restrictions which, if interpreted literally, could prevent or hinder your spare-time work. It will probably be as well to get the consent of those concerned right at the outset—do not, however, forget that they may have objections or reservations that are entirely reasonable. Your landlord may feel that your carpentry business could create a fire hazard, the owners of the block of flats where you live may feel that a constant flow of customers will annoy the other occupants or lower the tone of the place.

Even if you are a freeholder, it will be as well to check your title deeds and make sure that they contain no restrictive covenants; in older houses especially, such things are not uncommon.

Insurance

Whatever the source of your spare-time income it will, unless your work is conducted entirely outside the home, probably in some respect or other invalidate your householder's policy. If in any doubt at all you should contact your insurer or broker. Much better to face up to a small additional premium now than to find that the insurance company won't pay up for the TV the burglar took because you had given a front door key to your lodger, or that your fire insurance is invalid because you had installed a kiln for your pottery work without telling the insurance company.

The same applies to your car. The special case of mini-cabs is dealt with on page 129, but almost any use of a car for business purposes, even if you are only driving to visit a customer, can be a breach of the normal private user's insurance.

It should, of course, go without saying that if your work involves you in purchasing expensive equipment or carrying stocks, you must make sure that they are fully insured—and that you understand the basis on which the insurer will pay up in the event of loss or damage, as with most things concerning insurance the policy may not mean quite what you or I assume it does.

VAT

It is unlikely that VAT will affect many spare-time businesses, but there are exceptions and you should at least know the ground rules. The world is divided by the VAT men (who, incidentally, work for the Customs and Excise, not the Inland Revenue) into two: the registered and the unregistered. As private individuals we are all unregistered, and although a sole trader may register as a business, his registered status applies only to his business transactions, not to his personal affairs. VAT is rather like the game of pass the parcel, the parcel in this case being a surcharge of 15 per cent (at the moment, the Chancellor can alter the rate at will) on the price of all goods subject to VAT. The game consists of the registered players passing this undesirable package from one to another until it reaches an unregistered player, where it stops. But to add interest and variety to an otherwise boring game, the VAT man can, to change the metaphor, feed some jokers into the pack in the form of zero rates, exempt goods and so forth.

To illustrate the point, take the paper that has gone into the production of this book. The forestry company that grew the trees sold them to a paper-mill at so much per ton plus VAT, and paid the VAT to the Customs and Excise. The paper-mill turned the wood into paper which it sold to a paper merchant at so much per ream plus VAT; it reclaimed the VAT it had paid the forestry company and paid over the VAT it had collected from the merchant. The merchant sold the paper to the publisher at so much per ream plus VAT, recovered the VAT it had paid the mill, and paid over the VAT it had collected from the publisher. The publisher reclaimed the VAT he had paid the merchant but, because books are zero rated, he did not charge VAT when he sold the book to a bookshop, nor did the bookshop charge you VAT. The net result of all this was nil: no one, the forestry company, the mill, the merchant, the publisher, the shop, you or the government has lost or gained a penny.

On the other hand if the paper had been sold by the merchant to a stationery manufacturer, then the process would have been repeated all the way down the line to you, an unregistered consumer, who would have ended up paying 15 per cent VAT on your writing pad. Of course, if your business was registered, and you had bought the pad for business use, then you, too, could reclaim the VAT leaving the government, once more, with nothing for its trouble.

The great divide in the VAT world comes at the point where a business sells more than £23,600 worth of goods a year. Above that figure, you *must* register; below it, you need not register. (If you are near the borderline, check with your accountant: the level at which registration becomes obligatory can depend on quarterly rather than annual sales.) Whether you choose to register or not, assuming your business is small enough to have the option, will depend upon what materials you buy, what goods you sell, who you buy from and who you sell to.

But, you may say, every business pays VAT on something, even if it is only petrol and stationery—why not register and get the advantage of reclaiming it? The problem is that if you register you will, unless your goods or services are zero rated or exempt, have to charge VAT to your customers. If they, in turn, are likely to be registered, then it makes little difference to them since they can reclaim the tax. But if you sell mainly to consumers then registration will, in effect, force you to raise your prices by 15 per cent. The complications are legion. You might, for example, think that a business involving food would at least be free of them since food carries no VAT. But if you are running a catering service then it probably is subject to VAT, and if you are supplying wine as well you are of course paying VAT on that. The pros and cons of registration are, in short, a subject in themselves, and one upon which you should probably consult your accountant.

There are two points which are worth making here for those who are registered, whether from choice or necessity. As explained above (page 59) you must ensure that your bookkeeping and accounting systems isolate the VAT element in all your dealings; you will have to make regular returns showing the VAT you have paid and are reclaiming and the VAT you have charged and are remitting; and you have to be prepared to back these up with full documentation for the Inspector. Second, it is vital to keep in mind that VAT becomes due not when you pay a bill or receive payment, but at the date of invoice. This means that any registered business will almost certainly find it necessary to keep daybooks and ledgers of purchases and sales as well as a cash book. VAT can also affect your cash flow, since you may be paying the tax to the Excise before your customer has paid you or, more happily, reclaiming it before you have paid your supplier's bill.

What's in a name?

Sole traders and partnerships do not have to register if they wish to trade under a name other than that of their owners. But they have to put their own name or the names of the partners on their notepaper and other business documents, in order that customers and suppliers may know with whom they are dealing. The only limitation on the choice of business name is that it should not be misleading, offensive or suggest an association which does not, in fact, exist. Thus, should you happen to run a saddlery business in Windsor, it will probably be in order to call yourself Windsor Saddlery, but the House of Windsor Saddlery might get you into trouble on all three grounds. The rules for a company are more stringent. All company names must be registered and approved by the Registrar of Companies, who will refuse to allow the use of a name which is already registered by another company, or is very similar to it. The only exception would be where you have an excellent claim on that particular title; for instance, if you happen to have been christened Henry Ford then the Registrar will probably agree that you can call your company Henry Ford Ltd, but even if you are in the business of repairing electric motors he will draw the line at the Ford Motor Company Ltd.

Whether you adopt a trade name or not will depend upon your taste, your business, and your own name. If you have been christened Charles Chippit then you would do well to call your china repair business something else. A trade name gives scope for advertising and the building up of an image; but do not overdo it—customers could be disillusioned when they discover that the corporate headquarters of Global Ceramic Refurbishers is Mr Chippit's back bedroom.

Part II
A Directory of
Opportunities

6. Working for Yourself – a Second Income from Your Training, Trade or Profession

This chapter deals with the opportunities for earning a spare-time income by doing, on your own account, the same sort of work as you do for your employer in your trade or profession. It is clearly impossible to go into great detail, if only because the range of possibilities is so great, and it is also unnecessary since you will obviously already know a great deal about the field in which you earn your living. Much of the material is therefore more general than in other chapters, except for a few instances, such as bookkeeping or home typing, where it may be possible for those who are untrained to gain sufficient skill and experience to undertake spare-time work.

The professions

There are, of course, many professions which do not lend themselves to spare-time work: one can hardly be a spare-time brain surgeon or defend criminals in court over the weekend. Nor, if a professional is self-employed or a member of a partnership, is there any point in distinguishing between full-time and spare-time income if both are earned from the same work. But the architect or accountant, say, who is employed by a large firm or local authority may well find profitable opportunities for private practice. Provided that he is properly qualified and that his contract of employment does not forbid it, there is nothing unprofessional about such work.

If you are planning to do some spare-time private practice, there are two important points to remember. First, however little and sporadic the work, you are involved in a professional relationship with your clients, and if your full-time job does not involve you in the niceties of such relationships, it is prudent to check with the professional body in your field to make sure that you fully understand the responsibilities you are taking on. Second, you must make it quite clear to your clients that your work for them is a spare-time occupation and that they cannot, therefore, expect the same degree of attention as they would get from a full-time worker. A spare-time architect, for example, will have to arrange to inspect work or meet with builders outside normal working hours, a spare-time accountant cannot attend board meetings at three o'clock in the afternoon. Provided that such limitations are clearly spelled out from the start, they should pose no real problem.

Your scale of charges will almost certainly be more modest than would be the case if you were charging for full-time work, but do check any recommendations or requirements that may be laid down by your professional body—when it comes to fees some professional bodies operate systems of restrictive practice that would make the most militant trade unionist turn green with envy! In the case of most professions you will probably charge on the basis of the time involved in a job and, if your full-time employer charges for your time on the same basis, then the hourly rate he sets for your time will give you a useful guideline.

The most likely source of work will almost certainly be word of mouth recommendation—in the case of many professionals, advertising one's services is, in any case, prohibited. You will, of course, have to be extremely scrupulous about any work that may come to you as a result of contacts made through your full-time work: while your employer may well be delighted for you to do odd jobs for his clients which are too small or fiddly for him, he will rightly feel aggrieved if there is any suggestion that you are using his time and reputation to obtain private work.

Hourly earnings: £20 to £25 an hour is probably a reasonable charge for the time of most professional people.

Car: Likely to be essential.

Time and commitment: Pretty flexible, but once you have taken on a particular job you are naturally committed to seeing it through.

Start-up costs: Minimal in most cases.

Bookkeeping

This is a very fertile field indeed for the spare-time worker who has the proper qualifications, and even for those who are un-trained but have the time and energy to master accountancy practice and take the exams. There may well be courses available at your local evening institute and books on the subject are legion. As a bookkeeper you are not a professional accountant, and are not qualified to advise your customers or to audit their books of account; what you are doing is keeping a proper record of their business transactions in a form that will satisfy the Inland Revenue and enable their professional accountants to produce annual accounts with as little trouble as possible. Essentially, you are doing for the small business the work that, in a larger organisation, would be performed by an accounts department.

The demand for bookkeeping services is colossal: small shops and businesses, farmers, even other spare-time earners. Many, of course, do their own bookkeeping, but there are others who operate on the principle that any letter in a brown envelope should be stacked in a pile until the bookkeeper comes to sort it out. Probably the best way to find work at the outset is simply to ask around; though if you can make contact with local firms of accountants they may well recommend your services to some of their clients—provided, of course, that they feel your work merits their recommendations.

In most cases, you will find it best to arrange a regular monthly session with each client, either going to his premises or collecting the monthly batch of paper and doing the work at home. If, as will almost certainly be the case in many instances, you actually keep customers' books and records in your home you will obviously need a room in which to work and space for a filing system. You should also investigate the possibility of buying a fire-resistant cabinet in which to keep the basic records without which it would be impossible to reconstruct your customers' affairs, should there be a fire in your home.

Hourly earnings: £4-£8.50 per hour, with rates varying in different parts of the country, are the usual minimum charges for basic bookkeeping (eg bank reconciliation work). For anything more complicated you can charge higher rates—£12-£15 an hour would be fairly typical.

Car: Since you will have to visit each customer at least once a month, often taking heavy ledgers and files, a car is almost essential.

Time and commitment: The time you have to spend on the work will depend upon the number of customers you take on; but however few these may be you have a commitment to give them a regular and reliable service.

Start-up costs: Perhaps £150-£250 for filing cabinets, etc.

Typing

The kind of home typing work you seek will depend largely upon where you live. If your home is in a large town, with plenty of offices and businesses nearby, then it will be possible to offer an audio-typing service to, for example, small firms or individual professionals, who do not have full-time secretarial staff. But, clearly, speed is important if you are typing correspondence, and if you live out of town and are going to depend on the Post Office to carry work to and from customers, or take advantage of a weekly trip into town to deliver and collect it, then you will have to look for longer, copy-typing jobs where the turn-round time is less important.

Whether you use a manual, electric or electronic typewriter or word-processor will depend on how extensive your service will be and what kind of typing work you plan to do. A manual typewriter may be sufficient if you intend to spend only a few hours a week typing envelopes; for anything more than this (for example, invoices, business letters, CVs, theses) you will need either to buy or hire an office-size electric or electronic typewriter. Alternatively, you may wish to invest in a microcomputer with printer and word-processing software. The cheaper models, such as the Amstrad range, now cost little more (sometimes even less) than a reasonable electric or electronic typewriter, and they incorporate many features which will speed up and improve your efficiency. Word-processing is most effective for work where you are asked to produce a number of drafts of the same document or where you are frequently required to type a 'standard' letter (possibly with slight variations). It can also save a great deal of time if you have a list of addresses to which you regularly send letters and/or labels; the list can be stored on disc and your letters and labels printed out with a minimum of effort, without the need for repetitive copying.

If you are not already familiar with word-processing, you could test the water by enrolling on a short course, before you decide whether to buy a machine.

The best way of finding work is, in most cases, through small classified advertisements; and in the case of correspondence or other work for neighbouring businesses, in the local paper or shop windows. If you are looking further afield, advertising in literary journals, professional and trade magazines, etc, may be worthwhile. If you have experience or qualifications in particular fields, do use them. An engineer or a chemist will naturally feel happier having his reports or papers typed by someone who realises that RSJ is a girder and not a character from *Dallas*, or that a retort is a container as well as a reply. Legal and financial experience is particularly useful and if you have experience of professional typing work in either field you can certainly charge a premium for your services.

In the case of most work you will find it best to charge an hourly rate, but for long copy-typing jobs (book manuscripts, etc) it may be preferable to charge so much per 1000 words. Your fee will include the costs of paper and a single carbon or other form of copy; if a client wants additional copies you should charge extra. If you type correspondence under a client's letter-head then he will, of course, supply the stationery.

Hourly earnings: £3-£6, depending on where you live; you may be able to charge more in London.

Car: Not necessary unless you are going to have to collect and deliver work regularly.

Time and commitment: Typing can be taken up and dropped reasonably easily without disastrous consequences, so the work can be fitted in around other commitments.

Start-up costs: Nil (if you already have a typewriter) to £1000 or more if you plan to invest in one of the more sophisticated micros with word-processing software.

Further information: Running Your Own Typing Service (Kogan Page).

Consultancy

'If you can't do it', runs the adage, 'teach it'. To which one is tempted to add, 'and if you can't teach it either, be a consultant on it'. It is naturally unlikely that you will find much work as a consultant in any field unless you already have some reputation in that area (cynics would say that a reputation is *all* you need), so this is not an opportunity to any but the successful and established, but it can be a very well worthwhile one if you qualify.

The areas in which consultants tend to be most in demand are those fields of business which have gained in status or influence without having, at the same time, acquired any clear professional structure—if you have a tax problem you go to an accountant; if your office is falling down, to a surveyor; if you have a legal problem, to a lawyer; but if you have problems in sales management, distribution or computing you probably go to a consultant. Consultants are usually appointed to advise on or oversee a particular problem or project—to lay out a warehouse, for example, or computerise a particular operation. They are normally paid a flat fee for their services which can vary from simply writing a report to actually supervising a complete project. The size of the fee is quite simply a matter of what the traffic will bear: some feel that the basis that many professional full-time consultants operate on is to pull a figure out of a hat—and then double it. The major management consultants charge rates of £700 a day and upwards; operating on a spare-time basis, you are most unlikely to attract fees on this scale. Charging an excessively low rate in comparison to the market in general, on the other hand, may undermine your credentials and give the impression that you are simply not operating on a professional basis.

If you decide to undertake spare-time consultancy work you will almost certainly be trading upon the expertise you have acquired in the course of your full-time employment, and this can lead to tricky situations. Your boss may not be very happy to hear that you have taken all the hard won and expensively acquired experience you obtained when you reorganised the company's internal paperwork and sold it to his biggest rival— he may suggest that you remove yourself as well as your knowledge. So be careful and do not plunge into commitments over a few drinks on Monday evening which you may find deeply awkward in the cold light of Tuesday morning. Remember, too, that if you do a consultancy job properly you are almost certainly going to receive a good deal of confidential information about the business you are advising, and if you want to get more jobs you must strictly respect that confidence.

There are political hazards in consultancy as well. The two commonest reasons for a firm bringing in a consultant are, either that the management is deeply split over what to do and hope an outsider can referee their battle, or that they know what they want to do but feel more confident if they have paid someone a fat fee to confirm their view. In either case the possibilities of the consultant making himself unpopular are obvious. Tact is a prerequisite for the job.

Getting consultancy work is probably going to be a matter of keeping your contacts up to date and in good running order. You can, however, spread your reputation and improve your chances by writing and lecturing on your subject within your trade or profession and generally becoming established as an authority in your particular field. Potential clients are going to feel that much more confident that the consultant can simplify their internal paperwork if he is not just Mr Randall, but David Randall who has a monthly column in *The Journal of Office Management* and the author of that invaluable work, *Randall on Memoranda*.

How you calculate your fees is a matter between you and your conscience; with experience you will obviously be able to assess how much time a job is likely to involve, and what the market will bear.

Hourly earnings: See above.

Car: Useful, but may not be essential.

Time and commitment: By its very nature spare-time consultancy work is likely to be irregular and sporadic, but when you do take on a job it will probably involve quite intensive work for a short period.

Start-up costs: Nil.

Further Information: Start and Run a Profitable Consultancy Business (Kogan Page).

Design

In the worlds of graphic design, commercial art and typography, the freelance worker is king. Everyone involved is always doing some spare-time work to supplement their full-time income, or taking a full-time job for a bit when their free-lance work is at a low ebb, so this is a field where it is often hard to tell who is working in their spare time and who is full time. If

111

you already work in the field you will certainly be aware of this aspect, and you will also probably have gained a pretty good idea of where and how to come by spare-time work. Local advertisements, cards in shop windows, contacts with printers and advertisers are all sources of work and if your high street, like so many others, now boasts a fast print centre (they are never just shops, always 'centres') it will be worth your while to cultivate the acquaintance of the manager who probably has a large number of small design jobs to farm out. Advertising agents often use outside designers as do book publishers and some small magazines. The difficulty is, of course, that it is a very overcrowded field and an extremely competitive one.

The best way to maintain a regular supply of work is probably to specialise—in designing book jackets, for example, or business stationery, or posters. In this way you will become well established in a limited field, with your work coming from a restricted number of contacts, thus freeing you from the need constantly to seek new sources of work. As far as the competition goes, all that can be said is that design is a field always open to innovation and new ideas and one in which talent is quickly spotted and rewarded. You, obviously, have to supply the talent.

Hourly earnings: Depends on where you are, your experience and skills. A full-time professional freelance designer could be earning £20-£25 an hour, but it is unlikely that the part-time beginner could charge as much.

Car: Unlikely to be vital.

Time and commitment: It is relatively easy to move in and out of freelance design work, but you will probably find it difficult to get all the work you need if you don't stay in pretty close touch with your customers.

Start-up costs: Negligible.

The building trades

It is a fact that, even with high unemployment, small builders in many parts of the country have more work than they can handle and fewer skilled men than they need. There is thus plenty of scope for spare-time work. Not everyone has the skill or the inclination to do it themselves, and the kind of small jobs that a spare-time worker can reasonably undertake are often too small for the full-time builders to show much interest.

Building is also a field in which some informal co-operation, if not a partnership, between spare-time workers with different skills can be very advantageous. You will get that much more work if, when you take on a decorating job, you can also introduce a mate who can take care of the rewiring and another who will cope with the carpentry.

Skilled workers in the building trades buy and maintain their own tools, but some initial investment in larger items of equipment such as step-ups, ladders, etc may be required. A light van, or at least the occasional use of one, will also be a great help.

Clearly the work you are seeking will be as near as possible to your home, so local advertising, cards in the windows of local shops, etc is probably the best means of finding it. Do not be over-ambitious about the nature of the jobs you take on; in the long run you will do better out of a succession of small jobs, swiftly and punctually completed, than out of a single undertaking which may be beyond your resources and which should have been tackled by a full-time professional.

You should familiarise yourself, if you do not already have the information, with local building regulations, etc. It is unlikely that many of the jobs which a spare-time enterprise can tackle will involve planning permission, but it is possible that some of them will require inspection and approval by the district surveyor, or the environmental health or borough engineer's department; it is a disservice to your customers and to your reputation if you fail to make sure that all you do is in order with officialdom, however tedious it may be.

You should insist, even if the customer does not, on preparing a written estimate for each job and securing his acceptance of it in writing; and any variations from that estimate, or extras to it, should also be agreed in writing. Do make it clear to the customer from the outset that yours is a spare-time business and give a realistic estimate of the time each job will take; builders appear to be a race of optimists where time is concerned, and customers will be delighted and surprised if you finish a job early whereas they will be annoyed and frustrated if you are over-sanguine at the start and end up running behind schedule. In working out your estimates you should aim to 'pay' yourself at least £50 a day (more if you have special skills), but remember that any building work involves quite a lot of unproductive time, fetching and carrying materials, paperwork, etc which you must allow for.

Hourly earnings: £6-£8 is a reasonable target.

Car: Essential. A station wagon or light van will be preferable.

Time and commitment: Substantial. Building work, especially the small jobs which will interest you, is labour intensive, and nothing will damage your reputation more than a failure to complete work on time.

Start-up costs: Nil to £1000 depending on the tools and equipment you already own.

Further information: Running Your Own Building Business (Kogan Page).

Electrical repairs

All 'mod cons' are a blessing until they go wrong, at which point they all too often become deeply inconvenient, since it frequently seems impossible to get them repaired. Who has not been infuriated to find that the man who comes to mend the washing machine, the vacuum cleaner, or the fridge simply advises that there is no choice but to buy a new one, spare parts being no longer available or so expensive to install that it would not be economic—the bill for this unhelpful advice is usually at least £20. There is scope here for the handyman, particularly one who is qualified to repair electrical appliances and who is willing to apply a bit more ingenuity and interest than the average service engineer.

The problem is, of course, and this is why the manufacturers and their agents are so uninterested in providing repair services, that the parts *are* often hard to come by and the work fiddly and time-consuming. So, though you can certainly count on a demand for your services, do not expect to make a fortune—putting a new element in old Mrs So-and-So's kettle may be a five-minute job, but tracking down the right element may involve a five-hour search.

You will almost certainly need a reasonably sized workshop, not only for your tools and workbench, but also because you will find it invaluable to build up a stock of bits and pieces. If you are going to tackle larger items of equipment such as cookers or fridges, a station wagon or van is also going to be essential.

The great art is, of course, the ability to judge what is and what is not reparable, and what will be involved in the job. Here you will have to rely on your own skill and experience—it will be better to err on the side of caution than to take on problematical jobs which turn out to be even more awkward than you had anticipated. In anything involving electricity, and especially appliances used—or misused—in the home, safety must be paramount; this is not an enterprise to be undertaken unless you are properly and fully qualified and know exactly what you are doing.

Hourly earnings: £6-£8 would be a reasonable target.

Car: Likely to be essential.

Time and commitment: You will need a good deal of spare time, and if you are to build up and maintain a steady business the commitment will have to be fairly constant, too.

Start-up costs: Nil to £1000 depending on how well equipped you already are.

Car maintenance

If you are never happier than when flat on your back underneath a sump, then it is perfectly possible to earn a good spare-time income doing maintenance and minor repair work for others; but the project should be approached with caution. It may not be the end of the world if you make a mistake in repairing your own cherished 1965 Cortina, but it could be the end of your savings if you meddle fatally with someone else's brand-new, turbocharged Porsche.

You will need a place to work, even if it is only your own garage. Using the street outside your front door as an impromptu parking lot and maintenance bay will not endear you to your neighbours, nor will it result in good workmanship. You will also need a fairly complete tool kit, including items such as jacks and, perhaps, a hoist, which even second-hand will not be cheap.

How easily you find work will depend very much on your neighbourhood garages: if there are one or more establishments nearby which offer a thorough and reasonably priced service, then you could find it hard; but if they are only glorified filling stations which can muster not much more than a screwdriver and a couple of spanners, then you should be in luck. If you already work as a motor mechanic you will, naturally, have to be very careful not to poach customers from your employer.

Hourly earnings: You should aim at £6-£8 an hour.

Car: Probably essential for collecting parts, etc.

Time and commitment: Given that the best way of ensuring a supply of work will be to 'look after' quite a number of vehicles, you are going to have to give up a good deal of time and make a long-term commitment.

Start-up costs: Unless you are already well-equipped, these could be £1000 plus.

Hairdressing

Hairdressing is a job that might have been invented for the spare-time worker. Many women prefer to have their hair done at home in the evening or weekend for a moderate charge rather than face the business of making appointments, making sure they get their favourite assistant, etc and then paying a hefty bill at the hairdressers in the high street.

The ticklish part of the business is building up a clientele. You obviously cannot lure away customers from your employer — not, that is, if you wish to remain employed — and since the hairdresser/client relationship is a personal one, the response to advertising may not be good. People naturally feel vulnerable inviting a total stranger into their home and letting him or her loose on their crowning glory. So you will probably have to reconcile yourself to a fairly long process, building up a clientele from a base of friends and relations who will spread the word.

However, two major categories of customer which are fairly easy to find are the elderly and the infirm. Your neighbour, who has his elderly and partially crippled mother living with him, will most likely be delighted to pay you a few pounds one night a week to shampoo and set his mother's hair. Or, if you are close to a community home for the aged, check with the matron or supervisor to see if the residents would like a freelance hairdresser. Likewise, women who are just home from hospital sometimes require hairdressing assistance for a number of weeks. And what about the mother who has just given birth and can't leave her baby?

As every hairdresser will know, there is a delicate balance to be struck between caution and daring in the business. You may know that it really would improve Mrs Frump's appearance if she abandoned the back-combed beehive that didn't really suit her even when she first adopted it in the early 60s, but, however satisfying it may be to your creative instincts, you won't keep her custom for long if you adorn her head with that marvellous new style that you saw in last month's *Vogue*—it may be all the rage in the Champs Elysées but in Chipping Sodbury it looks plain daft. So remember, you have your customers' vanity and social standing as well as their hair in your hands. If your work makes them feel better about themselves, and their friends and neighbours envious, then you have not only kept one client, but you have also probably gained some more as well.

You will, obviously, need some equipment (several varieties of scissors, heated brushes, rollers, hairdryer, etc) but not a great deal more than you are likely to possess in any case. A car, however, is probably going to be vital, especially as you are most likely to find your customers away from the town or city centres in areas where a trip to the high street hairdresser involves something of an expedition.

Hourly earnings: You should probably aim for £4-£5 an hour.

Car: Likely to be vital.

Time and commitment: The time involved depends on how large a clientele you take on, but if you are to be successful your commitment to that clientele must be regular and reliable.

Start-up costs: Negligible.

Further information: Running Your Own Hairdressing Salon (Kogan Page).

Teaching

If you have professional qualifications or a skilled trade (again, with appropriate qualifications) there is a good chance that you can earn a spare-time income passing your knowledge on. The same applies to qualifications gained in the past which you are not necessarily using in your full-time job—that notoriously useless arts degree, for example.

The opportunities in schools are limited: first, of course, by the fact that the work has to be done in school hours which do not coincide with many people's spare time, but also by the fact that schools will only call on outside help where the subject concerned is one they cannot cope with from the resources of their own staff. The most obvious examples are instruction on certain musical instruments, the less common foreign languages and perhaps the practical subjects such as wood or metal work. Science and maths teachers are in great demand. But as secondary schools have become fewer and larger, and arrangements for the sharing of teachers and resources more elaborate, the opportunities for spare-time workers have diminished. The best openings will probably be found in the remote areas, where there are fewer schools and thus less chance of the education authority being able to meet all its needs with full-time staff. You will, clearly, have to show that you are fully qualified for the work and if you have past teaching experience or, for instance, a teaching diploma, that will weigh heavily in your favour. There is certainly nothing to be lost by making enquiries with head teachers or the local education office if you think you have something to offer.

The same limitations apply to spare-time work in universities, polytechnics or colleges of further education. The hours involved may not be spare from your point of view and the requirement is only likely to exist in what will be, from the institution's point of view, fringe subjects. But if you live near a university which has an extramural department or which runs summer schools, it is worth enquiring about opportunities there.

Much the best hope of regular work lies with evening institutes and youth centres. By definition, these operate outside normal working hours and rely almost entirely upon spare- or part-time teachers or instructors.

Evening institutes are run by the local education authority, usually making use of existing school premises, and many offer an almost bewildering variety of courses ranging from academic subjects to crafts or hobbies. In London a complete list of available courses is published each year in *Floodlight* and most education authorities will produce a similar list on request. Do not be put off if the subject in which you are qualified is not included—that may simply mean that they haven't found you yet! An enquiry at the nearest education office will put you in touch with the officer responsible for adult education in your district and you can take it from there. Understandably, the authority will want to establish that you are qualified and may also want to discover if there is a demand for the course you could offer, so do not expect an instant reaction; moreover, most courses start in September and the programme for the next 12 months is settled well before that, so you may find yourself too late for the immediate term.

The fees paid by students do not cover the costs of the service, which is paid for out of public funds, so the authority will be reluctant to sponsor a course which is unlikely to attract more than a handful of students; you will, therefore, be well advised to do some research to discover what subjects are already being taught in your area and, perhaps, how the range compares with what is available elsewhere. Forewarned can be forearmed.

If you do persuade your authority to give your course a try, you will find that they pay you according to a set hourly rate, and this, of course, assumes that you will spend time preparing outside the classroom as well as teaching inside it.

Youth centres concentrate on subjects with a recreational aspect—music and sports in the main. Again, they are the responsibility of the local education authority and you should start by enquiring at your nearest centre or at the education office. The work is often seen as social welfare for the young and the rates of pay reflect this; on the other hand, the rewards of working with young people can be high in terms of personal involvement and satisfaction.

A final possibility is the Workers' Educational Association. This charitable body has numbered such luminaries as R H Tawney among its staff in the past and offers evening courses in academic subjects mainly with a socio-political angle—members of the Monday Club will probably not find the work or the students congenial. If you think you have something to offer you should contact the nearest branch or, if there is not one, the central office at 9 Upper Berkeley Street, London W1H 8BY. Again, you should be aware that the WEA assumes that its lecturers have an interest in the work which goes beyond the purely financial one, and their rates reflect this.

Hourly earnings: Variable, depending on what and where you teach.

Car: Some form of transport will probably be essential. You may find the work involves travelling quite long distances late in the evening when public transport is not at its best.

Time and commitment: The time taken will depend upon the amount of work you need or find, but once you undertake to teach a course the commitment will probably be for at least 12 months.

Start-up costs: Nil.

7. House, Garden and Car

For most owner-occupiers, their house is far and away their most valuable possession, and it is therefore reasonable to consider if, by taking in lodgers or paying guests, it cannot contribute to the family budget. There is, however, one point that should not be dismissed lightly; taking strangers into your home will change the way you and your family live to some extent, although it need not necessarily be for the worse. No visitor will expect your family to behave like the staff of a five-star hotel, but they are entitled to protection from hazards you may have become accustomed to—rehearsals of the rock group your teenage son has founded, say, or your large Alsation who is so good with the kids but goes for strangers like a rabid wolf. Of course, you *may* find a lodger who is a virtuoso on the moog synthesizer and a man in whose presence lions cower, in which case all will be well.

Taking in lodgers

Provided that you have no more than six lodgers, there is absolutely nothing to stop you opening for business tomorrow. With more than six, you become subject to legislation which requires the inspection of your fire precautions and means of escape and may involve expensive alterations. You must, however, check your insurance policies and make sure you are covered for all contingencies; insurance companies or brokers will advise you on this. Normally, you will be expected to provide a lodger with a room and basic furniture, together with access to bathroom and, if separate cooking facilities are not provided, kitchen. Some landlords provide towels and linen, and keep them laundered, others do not. Obviously, such additional items, together with amenities such as a TV, will be reflected in your prices.

The lodger-landlord relationship can run the whole gamut from strict formality to honorary membership of the family—it all depends on the parties concerned. It will, however, be best to keep business relations businesslike, so do have a rent book for each lodger and insist on the rent being paid promptly and recorded properly, and make clear at the start any ground rules you are going to insist on. It would be a rare landlord today who insisted on a lodger being in by a certain hour or refused to issue a front door key; some may think it churlish to forbid a girl or boyfriend to stay the occasional night, but there does come a point where the line will have to be drawn and things will work better if you state at the outset where you intend to draw yours. If you provide use of a kitchen or bathroom in common then you certainly expect that they be kept clean and tidy. The same of course goes for you and your family—the lodger no more wants to find the bath full of your daughter's underwear than you want to find the fridge full of his stale food. You will also, if you are wise, make it a rule to have some parts of the house which are reserved for the family; however much you like your lodgers and enjoy their company there will be times when you want to be alone and the best way of achieving this without awkwardness or hurt feelings is to let it be understood that your living room, for instance, is your exclusive territory.

How easy it is to fill your spare room or rooms will mostly depend on where you live. A university, college or other institution such as a teaching hospital which attracts young unattached and relatively poor people to the district is almost certain to create demands for rooms to let. Most such places have an office or official who is responsible for putting would-be lodgers in touch with landlords and for vetting the accommodation you offer and the prices you charge. In the absence of such institutions, advertisements in the local paper, cards in shop windows or on the noticeboards of large offices or factories may produce results. Whatever you do, do not accept a lodger without first meeting him. You should also insist upon his inspecting the room and facilities before any deal is struck. And do not feel embarrassed about being choosy: there is no obligation at all to accept someone you dislike or feel uneasy about.

How much you charge will depend upon where you are and what you offer. In addition to the amenities already mentioned, for example, some landlords, especially those catering mainly for students, will provide breakfast and perhaps an evening meal as well. Current rates vary from £35-£40 a week in outer London, for a single room with shared use of kitchen and bathroom, to £25-£35 a week in a provincial university town with breakfast and dinner provided. If, like many, you accept a lower rent in exchange for babysitting or other services, then this arrangement should be spelled out and stuck to, although a good deal of give and take will be possible once you have got to know each other. One hazard to bear in mind: if you do not provide at least one meal a day, your lodgers come under the provisions of the Rent Act and have at least some security of tenure. This could not only result in your becoming stuck with a tenant you dislike, it could also cause problems should you wish to sell your house.

Hourly earnings: Assuming that it costs you between one and five hours a week in time per lodger (depending upon whether you are having to cook for extra mouths), the return on your time may be £4-£6. But you must also take into account the fact that lodgers are occupying space that costs you money, in terms of a mortgage or the profit you might show by moving to a smaller house.

Car: Not necessary.

Time and commitment: The commitment is a major one, not so much in terms of house as of adaptation to a novel situation; unless you are providing meals, the time involved will not be a major consideration.

Start-up costs: If you do not already have furniture for the rooms you intend to let these could be of the order of £150-£300 per lodger; extra linen, etc may have to be purchased, but those items apart, costs will be negligible unless you are embarking on the business in a big way with more than one or two lodgers.

Bed and breakfast

If you live in an area which attracts tourists, offering bed and breakfast is a possible alternative to taking in lodgers, but the income will, of course, be limited to the tourist season. As with lodgers, you are limited to no more than six guests if you cannot meet the stringent fire regulations which apply to larger establishments. And, in the same way, insurance cover must be checked. You will also, with a constantly changing population, require a good deal of spare linen, probably a large fridge or freezer, extra cooking utensils, etc.

In popular districts, it is perfectly possible to attract all the custom you need with one or two strategically placed signs, but it would be courteous, as well as saving yourself a good deal of trouble, if these are so arranged that you can cover them or change them when you are fully booked. The regional tourist boards publish lists of recommended guest houses and bed and breakfast establishments, graded according to the amenities provided (is there a separate bathroom with each room? is TV available? etc). In order to be included in these guides, you will have to pass inspection by the board concerned to establish that your accommodation is up to their strict (but entirely reasonable) standards. If there is a tourist information centre nearby you should make sure that the staff are aware of your existence and it may also be worth making yourself known to local hotels: they will probably welcome some alternatives to offer to weary and persistent travellers when they find themselves booked up. If it is at all difficult to find your house, do make sure that your signs are clear; it may be worth printing some cards with a sketch map which can be distributed to people who may pass visitors on to you. Do bear in mind that many of your guests may be foreigners who cannot be expected to cope with instructions like: 'bear left at the five-barred gate and then straight on for ¾ of a mile to the copper beech on the right.'—'*Faites attention, François. A gauche, dans une cage avec cinq bars, un ours? A droite, une plage, couleur de cuivre? C'est curieux, non? L'Angleterre.*'

It is not difficult to provide a few personal touches by keeping a stock of local maps and guide books, phone numbers for hotels and restaurants, garages, etc, which will help your guests. If people enjoy their stay many will return year after year, simplifying your work and, perhaps, gaining you a far-flung network of friends. The rates you charge will depend a good deal on the kind of accommodation you offer and the area in which you live and would probably range from £8 to £20 per person, per night.

You will, of course, need a reasonably sized dining room which will hold your maximum quota of guests comfortably, a reserve of crockery, cutlery and table linen, etc. Many bed and breakfast establishments also offer evening meals, and even packed lunches, especially in remote areas where getting dinner may not be a matter of a short walk down the street.

124

You should also take into account that many visitors are likely to have children; a collapsible cot or two which can quickly be installed in one of the rooms will come in handy, and if you have enough space, a swing and a few toys in the garden will almost certainly be welcome.

Hourly earnings: £5-£8 depending on your rates and the number of rooms you have available.

Car: Not essential.

Time and commitment: Two or three hours' work a day will probably be involved in the average household, more if you plan to offer evening meals. The commitment is a serious one: your business will certainly suffer if you close down for two weeks at the height of the tourist season for your own holiday, for instance.

Start-up costs: Ranging from, perhaps, £100 upwards depending upon the number of rooms available and how much spare household gear you already have.

Further information: Running Your Own Bed and Breakfast (Piatkus).

Farm holidays

Farm holidays are an elaboration of the bed and breakfast theme, with the difference that you are not dependent on passing trade and that you offer a unique type of holiday entertainment. (Farming may not seem much like entertainment to you when you are lambing in a foot of snow in February, but haymaking and calf feeding seem fun to the town dweller in the summer.) The one prerequisite is, of course, that you live on a farm.

An annual guide to farm holidays, *The Farm Holiday Guide*, is published by FHG Publications, Abbey Mill Business Centre, Seedhill, Paisley PA1 1JN, and inclusion in this is probably the easiest way of publicising your vacancies. Normally, visitors will come for a week or a fortnight and will expect accommodation with 'all found' in the way of food and facilities. How you arrange matters will depend on what you have available; holiday-makers may stay in the farm house, for example, and eat with the family or, if you have cottages to spare, you may offer self-catering holidays. Extras like pony trekking, fishing and so forth will obviously add to the attractions, but may increase your costs considerably.

You will have to be very clear about the ground rules. The fact that they are staying on a working farm is an important part of the attraction for many holiday-makers, and they will want to see what goes on, perhaps even lend a hand (though this should not be counted on); but you have to take into account the fact that you have a job to do and that farms can be dangerous places for the inexperienced. Do establish a clear set of rules especially for children, and also for yourself and your staff. If you leave a tractor standing about with the engine running you are just as irresponsible as the parent who allows little Johnny to poke the bull with a pitchfork. Like most things on the farm, running holidays is going to involve all the family and the staff, so you must make sure that all concerned understand what is involved and what is expected of them.

Rates vary a good deal with the desirability of your area and the additional facilities you can offer. In 1989 the scale runs from £8-£20 per person per night.

Hourly earnings: Not really applicable. You will have to calculate the amount of time involved in your particular case.

Car: It will be a rare farm that manages without one.

Time and commitment: The majority of the time is going to be involved in cooking, cleaning, etc. But the commitment involves the whole farm and must be weighed up on that basis.

Start-up costs: These could be considerable. Obviously, the level of comfort you provide and the amenities you offer will have to be substantially greater than the bed and breakfast minimum.

Selling garden produce

It is almost certainly a vain hope to imagine that you can make a significant and steady income from the usual fruit and vegetables produced even in a large garden. When you have more strawberries than you can cope with, they are probably dirt cheap in the shops as well and the pick-your-own merchant down the road has fields full. There may well be times when it is worth taking some surplus produce to a local market or even offering it to retailers, but these must be looked upon as rare bonuses rather than a planned source of spare-time income.

For those who hope that green fingers can produce extra cash, the best bet is a greenhouse, frames or cloches. Again, you won't be able to compete with the commercial growers when it comes to early or out-of-season produce, but bedding plants, pot plants, exotic flowers, etc can provide a worthwhile source of income. Unlike large-scale crops, they demand skill, attention and experience rather than a great deal of space, and these are things which you can provide as well as anyone. It follows that the more specialised and 'difficult' plants are likely to be the most financially rewarding. The gardener who has the skill needed to cultivate hot-house orchids will do better than the one who has to concentrate on tomato plants.

How you sell your produce will depend very much on what you grow and where you are. Local florists or garden centres should certainly be investigated, and many markets have stalls selling bedding-out and pot plants. If you go in for real exotica you are probably going to have to look further afield and make special arrangements for transport, etc. A lot of the skill will lie in building up a repertoire which provides you with a year-round income, or as near as you can get to one.

Unless you are fortunate enough to possess a large greenhouse already, the initial costs are likely to be pretty high; however great your ingenuity you will not make a lot of money from an eight by six foot greenhouse. In short, if you are seriously considering your garden as a source of income, you will have to plan in the long term and be prepared to invest a good deal of money. You will also have to bear in mind that the overheads can be high—fuel, pesticides and fertilisers, etc—and the risks fairly heavy—the market is a fickle one and subject to wild fluctuations in demand and price.

Hourly earnings: Very hard to calculate, but in costing your produce you should aim at £5-£6 an hour.

Car: Almost certainly essential.

Time and commitment: As any gardener will know, such a project will absorb all the spare time you have, and the commitment will have to be constant.

Start-up costs: Likely to run to four figures if you have to buy a greenhouse of worthwhile size.

Jobbing gardening

A particularly good bet in the suburbs and commuter belts around large cities where there are many large gardens whose owners have neither the time nor, often, the inclination to care for them themselves. Your clients' requirements can range from mowing the lawns once a fortnight in the summer to ensuring a year-round supply of vegetables and well-tended beds and borders. The usual arrangement will be to guarantee each customer so many hours' work per week on a regular basis, but do not forget that though you may be able to cope with ten or a dozen gardens easily enough in midwinter, the pressure is really going to be on in the spring sowing season when seeds and bedding plants have to go in, lawns need mowing and borders weeding.

An interest in and knowledge of gardening are clearly essential if you are to undertake more than the most basic tasks. Most people who have a medium-sized garden themselves will probably find that they have sufficient equipment to start out; tools such as spades, forks, hoes, etc are the basics. Some customers may supply you with them but you can't count on it and, in any case, everyone works faster and better with tools to which they are accustomed and which they care for themselves. Given that lawn-mowing is probably the job most in demand, a motor mower is a first priority, preferably a model with a grass box—Flymos may be fun but raking up the clippings is not. In due course if your business develops you may well find investment in other power tools, such as hedge clippers, even a cultivator, worthwhile. A car, preferably a station-wagon or light van, is virtually essential. Not only do you have to carry your equipment with you, but there will be supplies, some, like peat, pretty bulky, which require transport.

If you have a greenhouse or frames in your own garden, then there is no reason why you should not produce your own seedlings—vegetables, bedding plants, etc—for use in your customers' gardens, charging for these as you would if you had to buy them in from nurserymen. Your charges should be based on an hourly rate for your labour (£5 would currently be reasonable) plus the cost of supplies used. You have a choice here between supplying your own seeds, fertilisers, weedkillers, etc or getting each customer to purchase what you require for his garden. In the former case you may be able to benefit by bulk buying, but you will be involved in carrying expensive and often perishable stock. If you opt for asking your customers to make their own purchases, then remember that they will need plenty of advance notice, especially for items like seeds which may have to be ordered by mail.

If you can find your first one or two customers by personal contact then, experience suggests, word of mouth recommendations will soon bring you more work than you can cope with in many areas. Otherwise, an advertisement in your local paper, a card pinned up in your local garden suppliers, or a door-to-door canvass of likely looking households are good ways of getting work.

Gardening books are legion, and your local gardening club can be a useful source of information on local conditions and specialities, or even of potential customers.

Hourly earnings: Aim for £5.

Car: Essential in most cases.

Time and commitment: This will depend on the number of clients you take on and the nature of their gardens. It will also vary seasonally; but the commitment is a regular one, whatever the weather.

Start-up costs: Zero (if you already have the basic equipment) to £500.

Driving a mini-cab

If you own a car in reasonable condition and are prepared to work late hours you can consider using it as a mini-cab. Provided you do not 'ply for hire' but only pick up customers by appointment you require no special permit or licence; you will, however, have to change your insurance policy to include a 'hire and reward' provision which will cost an additional premium.

Most mini-cab and car hire firms rely to some extent on part-time drivers who supply their own vehicles, but you will find it impossible to get on to the books of a reputable company unless you have a clean licence. Initially, you may have to call in to get work, or hang about the firm's offices, but the larger and better organised businesses will usually supply two-way radios once they have ascertained that you are serious about the work. Rates, which are based on time and mileage, will be set by the company, who will take a commission on your earnings (you must, therefore, keep a careful record of trips and the sums charged); in the case of account customers the firm will collect the charges monthly and pay you your share after deducting commission. Tips can be pocketed, though you may find that your tax inspector will dispute your figure for these if it is unrealistically low. Petrol has to be paid for out of your own pocket, as do servicing and other costs. You will also have to make sure that your car is kept clean, inside and out, and in good running order.

This is probably not work for the nervous, as the demand for mini-cabs will be greatest late at night and the customers most likely to need one are either miles from public transport or have discovered that they are too drunk to drive themselves. You will, inevitably, encounter the occasional awkward or rowdy customer. The fares usually rise after midnight.

If you have spare time during the daylight hours, then you may find a car hire firm that needs drivers for more regular work such as taking customers to and from airports, etc.

Your local Yellow Pages will list mini-cab and car hire businesses and if you have a friendly local garage they may be able to give you the 'lowdown' on local firms. The rates charged vary, as does the amount of commission which the firms take; on average, after allowing for petrol and other costs you should probably aim to clear £3-£4 per hour worked provided you can keep fairly busy.

Hourly earnings: £3-£4.

Car: Essential.

Time and commitment: You will find it hard to get work and stay on a company's books unless you are prepared to work regularly.

Start-up costs: None, assuming you own a car.

Running a light removals service

This is an option only if you already own a light van. It is almost certainly not going to be economic to acquire such a vehicle solely for spare-time work. It is also unlikely to be a profitable undertaking unless you live in or near a large city with a fairly large population of young, mobile people. Your best chance of business lies with the flat dweller or lodger, who has too many possessions to get into a car but not enough to justify a proper removals lorry.

This is likely to be weekend work, and in many places, as a glance at the small ads will show, the competition is already stiff. However, the fact that so many are already in the business, and stay in it, suggests that the demand is there. A partner, or a friend who is willing to help out on a regular basis, will be a great advantage.

Hourly earnings: £7-£10.

Car: A van is clearly essential.

Time and commitment: A worthwhile income will probably necessitate working most weekends, and, if you have to travel any distance, working long hours.

Start-up costs: Negligible, provided you have a vehicle.

8. Kids' Stuff

Working with children can provide a wide variety of ways to earn money from home. Most communities and neighbourhoods have an increasing need for babysitters and childminders as more and more mothers enter into the full-time job market. And even those mothers who stay home to care for their children realise the need for well-run playgroups to provide stimulation and friendship for their children and a much-needed break for themselves. Giving private tuition, lessons, or doing part-time teaching are all ways to earn spare-time income while being involved with children, usually at a higher rate of pay than babysitting, childminding, or running a playgroup.

The first and foremost requirement for any of the jobs mentioned in this chapter is a genuine liking for and understanding of children: if you have a low toleration of noise, dirt, and general untidiness then a job involving young children is not for you. The jobs described in this chapter call for kindness, patience, and a highly developed sense of responsibility. You must never, for example, even consider leaving your charges alone if you are a childminder and you must remember that at all times children are dependent upon *you*. Most of the jobs covered in this section carry with them a heavy emotional commitment. In any case, working with children of any age group is physically hard, but for many people it is enjoyable and rewarding.

Babysitting

Babysitting, unlike childminding or working in a playgroup (see below), is not an activity which is regulated by local government. It means caring for children *in their own home*, with the consent of their parents, at an agreed hourly rate, usually at night.

There are two main ways in which you can obtain babysitting work. One is to register at one of the many agencies which seem to flourish in most large towns; the other is to spread the word through personal contacts, notices in your local tobacconist shop, etc.

The advantages of working through an agency are several: for one, it finds the work for you; another, it 'vets' you and provides you (as long as you stay with it) with a more or less permanent recommendation, so that you don't have to give references every time you work for a new family; and, in general, it demands slightly more than the going rate of pay for you. There are, however, some disadvantages. One is that you must pay the agency both a registration fee and a small part of your earnings. The other is that the people at the agency may well often send you out of your immediate neighbourhood; and, if you find a family for whom you really enjoy sitting, there is no guarantee that the agency will send you to them next time they need a sitter.

Most babysitters, in fact, get plenty of work by advertising themselves by word of mouth. Unless the family for whom you are going to sit knows you well, have ready the names, addresses, and phone numbers of at least two references. If you are still a student, for instance, one of your teachers, a neighbour or a vicar who knows you well will do. Remember, your potential employers are interested in your *human* qualities (are you responsible? are you good with children? etc) and couldn't care less if you are an Olympic weight-lifting champion or have a PhD in particle physics.

Say, for example, you notice that a couple with three children all under eight years old have just moved in across the street. You seize the opportunity to introduce yourself (with references in hand, of course) and volunteer your babysitting services. The chances are that you will be greeted as a saviour, but there are several points to remember which will both better the impression you make on them and make for a happy future relationship. The most important is to interest yourself in the children—it is they who are to be cared for. Another is to make a clear statement of your hourly rate and your times of availability. If, for instance, you hold down a full-time job and need your sleep, it is important to stress at the beginning that you must be home no later than midnight.

At this point, you may have impressed the family with your

responsibility and caring qualities; now you must ask yourself: are *they* a responsible family? Do they have a list, close to the phone, of 'emergency' numbers, as well as the address and number of where they are going? If you will be babysitting over supper, is there enough food for the children *and* you? Have they given you clear instructions about the children's bath and bed-time? Time is of the essence in your babysitting relationship: *you* must make sure that you always arrive on time; *they*, for their part, must be home when they say they will. Parents who are consistently late in returning home should be avoided.

Some warnings about babysitting. It is all too easy for babysitters to be exploited. Insist upon immediate payment for each job—and keep a careful log of the time you arrive and leave. Remember, you are there to take care of the children, *not* to do the housework. If that is expected, you must either refuse or request a higher rate for doing both jobs. It is wise never to babysit a sick child: it is unfair to expect you to carry such a heavy burden of responsibility and unfair to the child who requires, at this point, a full-time parent. Also, unless you have exceptional qualifications (nursing, teaching, social work experience, etc), avoid taking on children with special 'problems', physical or mental—without that vital training you can be running a risk for both the child and yourself. And, alas, problem parents (those, for example, you know or suspect have a drug or alcohol problem) turn out, in the long term, to be poor employers. Lastly, if the children you are tending are unruly to the point of making you feel like a matron in a borstal, then do move on to greener pastures.

Hourly earnings: Usually around £2 an hour, plus a lift home or your taxi fare. Do not hesitate to put up your rate in the case of special circumstances: ie more than two children, inconvenient hours, added housework, etc.

Car: A big advantage if you are going to take jobs outside your immediate area.

Time and commitment: As little, or as much, as you want.

Start-up costs: Zero.

Childminding

Childminding differs from babysitting, first and foremost, in that it is government regulated. You are a childminder if, for pay, you take into your own home one or more children (who are not related to you), five years old or under for an aggregate of two hours per day. Childminding is regulated by an Act of Parliament, and it is an offence to 'childmind' without being registered with your local council.

This said, childminding is an excellent way of earning money at home for a whole variety of people. If, for example, you are retired but wish to keep active without leaving your home a lot, then here is a perfect opportunity; or, if your own children have grown up and left the nest, childminding gives you the chance to keep yourself in touch with children without the heavy responsibility of fostering or adoption. Do you have a young child with whom you have to stay at home? Then childminding could be a way of earning money while carrying on raising your own child.

If you think you are interested in becoming a childminder, call the social services department of your local council. They will explain the rules and regulations concerning the job and, if you think you meet the standards and are still keen, they will send a social worker for a preliminary interview. You and your house must meet certain standards: most importantly, the social services department must assure themselves that you are a person suited to childminding. You must be healthy in body and mind, responsible, and not only be fond of children, but have some practical experience in caring for them. Your house or flat must meet certain hygienic standards, not be a fire hazard, provide a certain amount of floor space per child, etc. Social services will also check with the police that neither you nor any other adult in your household has committed offences relating to children.

Once you have been thoroughly 'vetted' and approved, your council will register you as a childminder. You will then discuss with a social worker what hours you would like to work. Remember, childminding does not have to be a full-time job— you are perfectly free to insist upon 'Mondays and Wednesdays only' or 'afternoons only'. It is you who negotiates with each parent your weekly or hourly pay, although the social worker will certainly give you some guidelines. Sometimes a parent's income is so low that she will not be able to afford your fee, in which case you will, in some areas, be given a supplement from the social services.

In the vast majority of cases, parents will find you through the social services, who hold a list of minders in the borough. It is up to you, in consultation with the social worker, to determine how many children you wish to care for at any time, and you may also take on children who do not come via the social services, though you must report their presence. A social worker will make occasional visits to see that all is running smoothly, and may be able to provide toys and safety equipment for your use.

Finally, do *not* consider becoming an unregistered childminder. The fine for the first offence is £50! The National Childminding Association, 8 Masons Hill, Bromley, Kent BR2 9EY, publishes pamphlets and advises on the law, insurance, etc.

Hourly earnings: Say, £1.50 per hour, per child.

Car: Not necessary.

Time and commitment: The number of hours you commit yourself to per day is up to you (the social services department will probably insist on at least two) and you can, of course, with proper warning, arrange breaks for your holiday, etc.

Start-up costs: You may want to invest in some toys, unbreakable dishes, etc.

Further information: Running Your Own Playgroup or Nursery (Kogan Page).

Playgroups

A playgroup may be defined, loosely, as a group of children under five years of age who get together for a few hours each day or several times a week for 'play' under adult supervision.

Playgroups are even more formally regulated than childminding, and it is therefore very worthwhile giving your local social services a call before beginning to set one up. Not only will you be heavily involved with social services, but town planning and the environmental health departments will most likely also get into the act—so it is best to get a good knowledge of all the various rules and regulations before doing any investigation on your own.

A great proportion of playgroups have their origins in two or more mothers wanting a more formal and stimulating agenda for their toddlers—as well as some spare-time cash. Running a playgroup can be an almost perfect spare-time profession for a mother of young children with some experience and qualifications in early childhood education. To make a playgroup financially viable as well as educationally and recreationally worthwhile, you must, of course, recruit enough children. This is best done through word of mouth, announcements in local church bulletins, or perhaps a notice in the local newspaper. Most playgroup leaders feel that they must have a minimum of at least five children per day to make all the effort worthwhile.

Next, you must find a suitable location. Because of the number of children for whom you will be caring, your home will probably be ruled out. This is where the advice and guidelines of the social services department will be invaluable. They will insist, for example, that any premises you come up with must have a certain number of interior square feet available per child, as well as a prescribed number of square feet of outdoor space; so many lavatories and wash basins for so many children; and, most importantly, so many adults for so many children.

It will take some time and research on your part to find a location which meets all the requirements. Try your local churches, which often have Sunday School facilities going unused during the week; and in this day and age, any church is delighted to pick up a little extra income. Also, with a shrinking school population, you might find some local primary schools with space to spare.

Once you, your staff and your premises have been vetted by the social services and other local authority departments, your playgroup will be officially registered. This, however, will not end your involvement with the authorities, who will keep a check on whether you are meeting their requirements. If, for example, you are serving lunch or a snack for your children, you must fulfil certain dietary and hygienic requirements. Your toys and equipment must be safe and clean.

Running a playgroup demands a great deal of record-keeping, and not only for financial purposes (see Chapter 3). You must keep a record of each child's immunisations and medical history, as well as the name and number of the family's GP. You will probably find it easiest to keep a file on each child: his name, date of birth, address, parents' employers, number of siblings, allergies, special problems, etc, since social services will want to see most of this information anyway. It is best to keep a 'log' for parents to sign when they bring their child and pick him up; you will find this will help you to avoid unpleasant and embarrassing scenes later on when payment is due.

What you charge each parent, either on an hourly or weekly basis, depends upon several factors. What can *they* afford? Are you in an inner-city area with high unemployment? Or is your playgroup situated in a comfortably well-off suburb? If you are in a rural area, will parents have to spend money on petrol simply to get their children to you? If you have very special qualifications (such as an MA in early childhood education), you can feel justified in charging more. Your social services department can give you excellent guidelines. In some areas, where there is a dearth of such facilities, you may even be entitled to a grant for toys, equipment, or food. The Pre-School Playgroups Association, 61-63 Kings Cross Road, London WC1X 9LL, publishes several useful leaflets and is a good source of information and contacts with those in the field.

Do, at this point, go back to Chapter 3—for running a playgroup is really like running a small business. Remember, you have to cover costs such as rent, toys, and food as well as pay yourself. Again, do not consider starting an unregistered (and therefore illegal) playgroup—the fines are stiff!

Hourly earnings: See above.

Time and commitment: Approximately 2-5 hours per day.

Start-up costs: You may have to invest several hundred pounds in toys and equipment, which may necessitate a bank overdraft or other forms of loan (see Chapter 3).

Further information: Running Your Own Playgroup or Nursery (Kogan Page).

Private tuition

This is an area which does not call for the intense emotional commitment demanded by caring for young children. You are, to put it simply, offering your professional skills on a freelance and, usually, one-to-one basis. The one real advantage in engaging in private tuition is that you can not only pick and choose your hours but, to some extent, your pupils. Giving private tuition is an excellent way of supplementing the income of qualified musicians and artists (see Chapter 9), as well as teachers and graduate students. Be sure, before seeking your students, to have the documents verifying your special qualifications or advanced training at hand; also, it's a good idea to have one or two personal references about.

Now, how do you advertise your services? Running a small classified advertisement in your local newspaper for a period of at least several weeks usually brings results—or, for much less expense, you can place a notice at your local newsagent and tobacconist. Make sure, however, that you state clearly in the advertisement your qualifications, your hourly charge, and the times at which the tuition is available. If there are private schools in your area, do write them a letter stating what tuition you can offer. You will, most likely, belong to a society (or union) which is devoted to your profession, and many carry registered rolls available to the public giving the names of their members qualified for the teaching of, say, chemistry. Many schools or sixth-form colleges have bulletin boards on which a notice can be placed.

Most private tutors prefer their pupils to come to them, in which case you must set aside a room which is quiet, orderly, and adapted to whatever it is that you teach; some parents, however, may insist that their child be tutored in his or her own home. Maintaining a good relationship with parents is of primary importance: you must settle upon a fair rate of pay and determine whether it is to be paid weekly or monthly (here again, good record-keeping is essential) and you must ascertain that you and the parents agree on the exact nature of the tuition.

You will have to accept that you will be very busy during certain times of the year, and not at all during others. 'Academic' tutoring involves its ups and downs in time and commitment, and at times you will be under a lot of pressure to 'cram' children into passing exams. On this last point, it is essential that you be firmly realistic with parents. It will do your reputation no good to promise miracles for a child who has not opened his textbook for eight months; parents may not only be disappointed with the dismal results, but may refuse to pay up fully because your promised miracle failed to come off.

If, however, you are able to offer guitar lessons to local teenagers, your spare-time working life may be a lot simpler and more regular. The chances are that, except for vacation periods, parents will want their children to see you on a regular, weekly basis. Again, do be honest with parents regarding their offspring's current and potential talent; and make sure that they understand that their child will also have to practise, as well as see you, to become competent.

What you charge depends upon your qualifications. Check with your own fellow professionals for going rates.

Hourly earnings: See above.

Car: Probably not essential.

Time and commitment: May fluctuate but, in general, as much or little as you want.

Start-up costs: Zero.

Organising classes, etc

A certain kind of private tuition cannot be given in your own or student's home. When your speciality involves a great deal of physical movement, as in judo, or special equipment, such as scuba-diving, then you will have to search for facilities.

Since you are thinking of running a class for spare-time income purposes and not looking, for example, to set up a school of ballet dancing, it will be most economical for you to search for an institution which will not only provide you with the space and equipment for your classes, but will advertise them and pay you directly, instead of your collecting from each student in your group.

Most inner-city and many rural areas have community centres which offer classes of all sorts, and which just may be looking for a teacher of your skills. Next, there are youth centres, which are always on the look-out for someone to teach new sports and recreations. Most areas now have large 'sports and leisure' centres offering a wide range of lessons—a quick trip to their personnel offices may be all you need to get your yoga classes going. And do check in your local Yellow Pages for various clubs which may have need of your services.

You may be asked to sign a simple contract if you choose to run classes for any of the above, simply stating that you will give X number of classes each week for X amount of time at X amount of pay per class, etc.

If, however, you decide to rent space and equipment for your own independent classes, do re-read Chapter 3. Remember, rental fees and insurance (if you are teaching some form of physical activity) can be expensive overheads which may well bite deeply into your profits—as well as provide more paperwork. Also, you must register yourself and your premises with your local council, which will provide guidelines as to safety and health factors.

Hourly earnings: Varies.

Car: Not essential.

Time and commitment: Variable.

Start-up costs: Rental of space and equipment may be substantial.

Part-time teaching

If what you teach is very specialised, then many schools may have use for you on a part-time basis. Music departments, for instance, in large schools may have a need for clarinet coaching once a week. Or, if you have special training and experience in teaching dyslexic children, then local primary schools may well want you to teach remedial reading for several hours a week.

There are two main ways in which to obtain part-time teaching jobs. One is to register with your local education authority; the other is to write to the private schools in your area stating your qualifications, experience, and the hours for which you are available. See also 'Teaching', pages 117-20.

Hourly earnings: Each local education authority has standard rates of pay for part-time teaching and most private schools pay comparable rates.

Car: Not essential but very desirable given that the work may involve travelling to several different schools.

Time and commitment: Varies.

Start-up costs: Zero.

9. Cooking and Sewing

Not so long ago it would have been almost universally assumed that a spare-time income from cooking or sewing was strictly a woman's province. Happily, things have changed, and men who fancy their chances with pastry knife or pinking shears should no more feel inhibited about making use of their talents than women should steer clear of work involving spanners or screwdrivers.

The immediate attraction of the opportunities offered by cooking or sewing is that the work can usually be done in the home and may demand only modest additions to the household's basic equipment. It is also a field in which the individuality and personal enthusiasm of the spare-time worker can give him a real edge over larger, full-time competitors. You will not be aiming to capture anything more than a tiny fraction of the vast market for food and clothes, but the fraction you have in your sights is the one that values quality, originality and individuality. So, whatever you make, you should always remember that quality is more important to you than quantity—the supermarket and the chain store are not interested in foodstuffs the manufacture of which cannot be mechanised or garments that have to be made to measure, but if you try to compete with them at mass production and mass marketing they will wipe the floor with you.

It should be noted that if you prepare food for sale in your own kitchen you are, technically, subject to the Food Hygiene Regulations. Your local environmental health department may want to send someone round to inspect your premises and he may insist on changes in equipment or practice. The inspector can hardly concern himself with everyone who sells a few jars of pickles at the church fête, but if you are intending to go into the home cooking or catering business on a regular basis you should get in touch with the Department at the outset and make sure you are able to comply with their regulations.

Cooking at home

If you plan to cook or prepare any kind of food in your home for sale to the public your first priority must be to establish that you have a means of selling it. With a few exceptions, the perishability of your produce will mean that the outlets for it have to be fairly close to home. High quality grocers and delicatessens are probably the most likely places to stock and sell the spare-time cook's produce, but restaurants, pubs, clubs and wine bars are other possibilities and if you have a good local market that, too, may provide a point of sale.

The logic of both production and sales is in favour of specialising in a fairly limited range. You are, as we shall see, almost certainly going to have to invest in some equipment and you will not want to buy more than you have to; nor will you want to spread your sales and promotion efforts wider than you need. The traditional staples of the spare-time cook have been things like pâté and quiche, sufficiently exotic in the 50s and 60s to command attention in a country where meat and two veg were the norm, but well within the range of the amateur cook. Whether or not your locality is already blasé about *pâté de campagne* and *quiche lorraine* only you can judge, but one alternative is to take advantage of the growing enthusiasm for British cooking. Cookery writers and gourmets have, of late, given British cuisine back some of its self-confidence and it is no longer axiomatic that all good food comes from the other side of the Channel. This trend certainly offers opportunities if you come from an area which has local specialities or is identified with some particular raw material—Devonshire cream or Scottish salmon would be cases in point. The food industry has done much to devalue things like Cornish pasties and Dundee cakes. Why not show that, properly made, they deserve to be treated as delicacies?

There is usually a market for well-made, superbly iced wedding and birthday cakes, if your expertise runs along these lines. The charge for a single tier can range from £15 to £50, depending on quality.

The freezer offers other opportunities. Unlike a professional, you will not be able to make daily deliveries of highly perishable items, but much produce can be stored for a week or more without ill-effects and without requiring vast amounts of freezer space. If you are going to buy materials in bulk then a freezer can also be essential for storing them. It would, of course, be idle to pretend that a worthwhile business can be built up on the basis of a kitchen the size of a large closet and a couple of hot-plates. You will need a decent-sized place to work and a set of equipment to match. Cooking a dozen pies should not be 12 times as much work as cooking one, but it will be unless you have the space and the utensils to work on a larger scale. You are also likely to find that a certain degree of mechanisation pays off—you lose nothing in quality when you replace a hand mincer with a food processor, but you save a lot in time and effort. The sort of equipment you need is more likely to come from a supplier to the catering or restaurant trade than from your local hardware shop.

You will probably have to rely on local retailers for your supplies, but in most cases your buying will be on a scale which entitles you to some discount. Don't be afraid to ask for this, although in return the shopkeeper is entitled to expect warning of your requirements and a willingness to fit in with his needs. For example, the butcher may be delighted to get your order for 20 pounds of sausage meat, but he won't be happy if you turn up and ask for it out of the blue when he's got a queue of customers waiting. Even if it takes a good deal of trial and error, you should aim to build up a list of regular suppliers who offer you consistent quality, reliable service and the right price.

Home cooking is a field where partnerships are particularly common and successful. This is in part because many who choose this source of spare-time income are mothers of school-age children whose free time coincides with school hours—a partner can provide company as well as help. Also, two cooks working together are likely to be more flexible and more productive than two working apart, and a pooling of equipment can be beneficial.

It should go without saying that, if you are producing any sort of foodstuff for sale, cleanliness and hygiene are of paramount importance.

Women's Institutes can be very helpful in this field: they issue certificates in some skills, offer short courses at their college in Oxfordshire and, in many areas, run regular market stalls for produce. Ask your local WI or write to the National Federation, 39 Eccleston Street, London SW1W 9NT.

Hourly earnings: These will vary enormously, but you should aim, when costing your produce, to 'pay' yourself at least £6 an hour. Remember the hours you work include shopping, preparation and cleaning up as well as cooking.

Car: Unless you are very conveniently situated you will almost certainly need a vehicle to deliver produce and collect materials.

Time and commitment: Cooking cannot be hurried if you are to achieve a high and consistent standard, and continuity will be important from the sales point of view. It will probably not be worth considering cooking at home unless you can spare a minimum of eight hours a week on a regular basis.

Start-up costs: These will vary, but unless you are prepared to invest £100 or more in equipment you are likely, in the long run, to be handicapping yourself considerably.

Cooking for office dining rooms

Directors' lunches range from affairs of great distinction and elegance, complete with white-coated butlers and decanters of port, to relatively informal and makeshift gatherings. The grander establishments may well employ a full-time chef, but more and more companies are aiming to entertain at a level equivalent to a good local restaurant, offering simple but interesting food and wine in informal surroundings. The dining room may be available to a regular group of senior managers and their guests every day, or may be open to all in the office who have to entertain luncheon guests as well as catering for small receptions and company occasions such as board meetings or sales conferences.

Obviously, this is a field where even the most skilful and energetic can work for only one master at a time so the office cook may well find her- or himself a part-time member of staff rather than self-employed (some firms, however, buy in cold and ready-made dishes rather than having their own kitchen. See under 'catering', page 148). However, if you are asked to cater on a freelance basis, you may wish to charge on a 'per head' basis. One freelance caterer in London, for instance, charges £16 per head (1989) for directors' lunches.

For the individual who enjoys cooking, relishes spending part of the day in an office setting, and is confident of maintaining a reasonably professional level of cooking and presentation, this can be an ideal opportunity. But it is also one beset with hazards for the unwary or the novice. You must make sure before committing yourself to any job that both you and the employer are clear about what it does and does not involve. Are you to do the shopping as well as the cooking? This will add at least an hour to each day's work, and lugging the materials for a luncheon for 12 back from the shops is not light work. Are you to serve the food yourself? And what about the washing up? Does the rest of the office use the kitchen as a coffee-making depot, leaving the debris for you to clear up? What sort of cooking is going to be required? If what they really want is meat and two veg day after day, then it may only involve an hour or two's work, but you may also be bored stiff if what you are longing to do is devote several hours to producing an elaborate meal of *quenelles de brochet*, followed by *perdrix au choux* and ending with *crème brûlée* and *petits fours*.

A properly equipped kitchen is essential with as much labour-saving equipment as possible; cooking a formal meal for a dozen, or even half a dozen, involves a great deal more work than the average family meal—it's more like giving a dinner party every day of the week. One point you must insist upon is that a single—and efficient—person in the office is appointed to liaise with you: it is no joke to be told when you have just bought steak for four that there are going to be six and one of them is a vegetarian and another a strict Hindu! You should try to ensure that you always have a minimum 24 hours' notice of how many you are catering for and what is required.

The only equipment you need bring to the job is your talent and enthusiasm. But if the place of work is miles from any decent shops then you will need a car and a reliable parking place—if not you must ensure that tradesmen can and will deliver. It is perfectly possible to cut down the amount of time you spend at the office by doing much of the preparation and cooking in your own kitchen. Many dishes can be pre-cooked or even stock-piled in the freezer without ill-effect. But take this into account when reckoning up your time and your fee.

This is not work to be undertaken if you are a slapdash or nervous cook. Your family may be understanding when the beef is cooked to a frazzle, but the managing director may not forgive you if you serve it up to his most important customer. And it takes calm nerves and a practised hand to cope when the guest of honour is half an hour late or a pre-lunch meeting drags on longer than expected, leaving you with the prospect of a ruined meal.

If you are going to have to purchase the food, and perhaps the wine too, then make sure that a clear budget is established and that everyone realises what you can and cannot achieve within its constraints. Some managers who would think nothing of spending £50 or £100 in a restaurant can be very unrealistic about the costs of preparing an equivalent meal in their own kitchen. Conversely, you must be careful to stay within the agreed budget. Most employers will expect you to keep receipts for all purchases, either reimbursing you on a daily or weekly basis or arranging for you to have a cash float.

If you are sufficiently experienced to undertake this work then you will probably already have a shelf full of cookbooks, but it may be worth acquiring a few more, designed for the professional rather than the amateur. Similarly, if you find yourself responsible for equipping the kitchen, or adding to its equipment, it will pay to visit, or obtain catalogues from, a shop specialising in professional catering equipment. The materials will be harder wearing, of better quality and easier to use than much of the stock in your local shops.

There are agencies which specialise in supplying cooks for this work and some cookery schools such as Cordon Bleu in London offer courses and also recommend pupils or ex-pupils to employers; many firms will advertise a vacancy in the local press and you can approach possible employers direct or, even better, through personal contacts.

Hourly earnings: Aim to charge at least £6 an hour; in London and the South-East you could probably charge more.

Car: Essential only in special cases.

Time and commitment: Between two and five hours a day perhaps, plus additional time working in your own kitchen at home. This is a regular, five days a week job, even if not eight hours a day.

Start-up costs: Zero.

Running a catering service

The first thing to be clear about is that the business of catering for large occasions such as wedding receptions where the caterer may be expected to provide crockery and cutlery, waiters and perhaps a marquee as well, is best left to the professionals.

There are, however, also opportunities to cater for smaller events and private parties, though these, too, present difficulties for the one-man or one-woman band. You will have to spread your net pretty wide to ensure a steady flow of business, and frustrating periods like Christmas, when you could do with half a dozen partners, will alternate with slack times. While the inventive cook can do a great deal, with the help of a freezer, to lay in stocks and make long-term preparations, much of the catering effort is inevitably a matter of the last few hours before the party. You also have to face up to the fact that your social life is going to suffer— when everyone else is feeling relaxed and sociable you are hard at work.

Fortunately, there are alternatives which offer more manageable and regular opportunities for the spare-time caterer. For example, many offices which do not run a dining room or cook (see previous entry) do, nonetheless, have working lunches, meetings or business get-togethers at which they would like to offer something a bit more distinctive than two rounds of corned beef sandwiches and a packet of crisps from the snack bar across the street. Half a dozen or more such firms can provide a steady flow of business ideally matched to spare-time work. You should insist on getting as much notice as possible of their requirements and you should establish one reliable contact in each office through whom these requirements are relayed.

On a less exalted level, many workers from offices and elsewhere would welcome a chance to get simple sandwiches and other snack lunches of more interest and quality than those provided by the average sandwich bar or pub. It will have come as a revelation to most British visitors to New York, for example, that it is possible, with a phone call to the nearest 'coffee shop', to conjure up any one of a hundred varieties of sandwich, made with a choice of bread and seldom less than four ingredients. One highly successful spare-time business has taken advantage of this gap in the market and works on a system of daily deliveries, with each customer giving an order for the next day's lunch when today's is delivered. If you live in or near some largish office blocks, this might be a very worthwhile possibility to investigate. Fresh bread, a choice of fillings and, perhaps, some pastries and fresh fruit should suggest a repertoire with which the skilful and interested cook can win a loyal clientele.

Another possibility, though more seasonal, is the provision of hampers and picnic meals. If you live in a tourist area or near a holiday resort then you might well find during the summer a steady demand for inventive and good quality picnic fare. There is also an obvious chance to link up with hotels and guest houses who, the evidence of many of their offerings suggests, do not much care about providing packed lunches for their guests.

As with home cooking of food for resale (see page 143), you are going to have to add to your kitchen equipment, but probably not on a very expensive scale; and if you are delivering sandwiches or packed meals, etc you will also have to take into account the materials needed to keep them fresh and presentable in transit.

Hourly earnings: Impossible to give any useful figures. £6 an hour is probably what you should be aiming for after covering all costs.

Car: Almost certainly essential.

Time and commitment: Success is going to depend on a steady flow of work; in many cases (a sandwich service, for example) you are going to have to fit into a daily routine. Remember, too, that if you cater for parties you are going to be the last one to be consulted about the time and the place, so be prepared for your life to be disrupted pretty often.

Start-up costs: Variable, but unlikely to be less than £250.

Further information: Running Your Own Catering Business (Kogan Page).

Dressmaking

In earning a spare-time income from dressmaking you can match your ambitions to your skill and talent. If you enjoy experiment and have a flair for designing and cutting material, then there is no reason why you should not design as well as make clothes. Even if you don't have the skill or the interest in design required for this, you can probably still find plenty of work making up clothes to the customer's own design or commercially available patterns.

The likelihood is, unless you have something really new and original to offer and can find a shop or boutique willing to back you, that you will get most of your work from private clients. There is a steady demand for clothes which are individualistic or even just sufficiently different to be noticed, and many women find that they have a length of material, perhaps silk from the January sales or tweed from a Scottish holiday, which they would like made up into a dress or coat and skirt with that little bit more professionalism than they themselves can manage.

In the long run this is a business in which word of mouth recommendation will count for more than anything else, so the sales problem often comes down to getting those first few jobs which will start the ball rolling. Small advertisements in the local press, contacts through friends or local women's groups, even perhaps a recommendation from the sales staff in a shop which sells fabrics can be a starting point.

If you are sufficiently proficient and experienced to be considering the work at all then it is likely that you already own an electric sewing machine, but you may well find, at the outset or fairly soon afterwards, that a bigger machine with more attachments will save time and give you more scope—if the capital outlay is a problem a reasonably steady work rate should make hire purchase a possibility. You will also, of course, need some other fairly inexpensive equipment and a stock of basic materials. But in most cases the more expensive materials will be provided by the customer, or specified by her, in which case you can reasonably ask for an initial deposit to cover the cost. You may also find it worthwhile to subscribe to one or two fashion magazines from which both you and your clients can get ideas.

This is work which can fairly easily be fitted into the routine of a busy household, but you must bear in mind that you will have a steady flow of customers calling for fittings, occasions that go more smoothly if they are not interrupted by children, or your husband looking for a sweater. The family will have to accept a little discipline and collaborate in ensuring that one room in the house is kept clean and tidy for callers.

Hourly earnings: You should aim at charging at least £5 an hour for your time.

Car: Probably not needed.

Time and commitment: Your working hours can be fairly flexible and, provided that you keep busy enough to retain a regular clientele, the commitment need not be one which interferes too much with your other work or interests.

Start-up costs: Zero to £250.

Knitting

If you are already a compulsive knitter, then you can certainly make use of your talent to earn a little money; but as a source of worthwhile income the work comes very low on the scale of preferences. The problem is that, whether you knit by hand or with a machine, you simply cannot compete with mass production methods—methods which are so sophisticated that they can, in most cases, match your quality at a far lower price.

Certainly, the investment involved in buying a knitting machine could not be justified by its potential as a source of additional income—unless you included on the credit side the savings you made by producing garments for yourself and your family and the satisfaction you gained from the work.

Hourly earnings: Most knitters aim to earn £2-£2.50 per hour.

Car: Not necessary.

Time and commitment: To earn anything more than pin money you would have to work very long hours indeed.

Start-up costs: Even second-hand, knitting machines are not cheap; new they run well over the £200 mark.

Ragtrade outwork

If you live in a city with a large clothing industry then you will know that the many small businesses which it comprises have a need for 'outworkers', people who make up the garments usually from materials already cut according to a pattern. Though this work is relatively easy to find, you should probably only take it on as a last resort. Apart from the fact that it is repetitive and boring, it is also extremely badly paid and even the nimblest and swiftest seamstress can probably do better working for private customers. One other word of warning: the ragtrade has

151

a higher rate of bankruptcy than any other industry, so if you do get involved, make sure you are paid regularly and on the dot.

The advantages of being an outworker are that it provides regular work, involves you in no major risk or sales effort, and that the sort of work concerned is usually fairly straightforward and elementary. Outwork is usually done on piece-work rates, that is, so much per garment or dozen items completed.

Hourly earnings: Around £2.

Car: Not necessary.

Time and commitment: It will not be worthwhile to an employer (or you) unless you can give several hours to the work most days, although in principle you can take on as little or as much work as you please.

Start-up costs: None (provided you already own a sewing machine).

Other sewing work

There are, of course, many other purposes for which your sewing machine can be used beyond dressmaking: curtains, loose covers and soft toys are obvious examples.

Curtains and loose covers are commodities for which it should not be difficult to find a ready market. As with dressmaking (with which they can be easily combined), personal recommendation is the most likely source of work; but if you have a local store with a substantial fabric department it may well be worthwhile contacting them as they may be willing to recommend you to their customers or, if they undertake making up work themselves, they may subcontract jobs to you. Remember, though, if you are making loose covers, at one stage or another you are going to have to go to the furniture or the furniture will have to come to you—except in cases where you are acting as a subcontractor to a supplier who can provide patterns.

The chances of making a steady income out of soft toys will probably depend upon whether you live within fairly easy reach of a toyshop which has a market for something a bit different from and a bit better than the mass produced goods which are on the market. One or two 'trendy' shops with a clientele of prosperous mums could keep you comfortably in business, but if your area boasts no such outlet you may find it a real struggle to make a worthwhile income.

Hourly earnings: Could be anything from £2 an hour upwards, but aim for a viable rate (eg, £6 an hour plus) when costing your work.

Car: May be needed for collecting and delivering materials and goods.

Time and commitment: This can be slow, painstaking work, so maintaining a steady flow of business could involve at least eight hours a week, but timing and commitment can be flexible.

Start-up costs: None (providing you already own a sewing machine).

Designing and selling clothes

If your ambitions extend to designing a range of clothes and selling them direct to customers you will probably have to go into the mail order business, and the costs involved in this are unlikely to be bearable unless they are spread over a fairly substantial output. So this is probably something to be embarked on only if you have one or more partners, or are in a position to employ others to do some of the work. The problem is that you are aiming at a general market, and so the magazines which serve it have large, general circulation and advertising rates to match; moreover, the nature of the goods themselves demands glossy, colour pictures so direct mail selling is also costly.

But if you do have the talent and the resources, this is a field full of success stories about those who have dared and won—no one, of course, hears about those who dared but lost—and there is no reason why your name should not be added to the list. The thing to bear in mind, however, is that if you are successful you are probably working your way towards a full-time business rather than a spare-time income, and that the kind of investment required and risk involved reflects that fact.

Hourly earnings: Impossible to quantify.

Car: If you subcontract work, or take parcels for dispatch, etc it is likely to be indispensable.

153

Time and commitment: You will not be going into this kind of venture unless you have a good deal of spare time and total commitment to success.

Start-up costs: Substantial, perhaps £3000-£7000.

10. Being Crafty: An Income From Your Craft or Hobby

In a single chapter—probably, indeed, in an entire book—it is not possible to cover the whole range of crafts and hobbies and the opportunities they offer for earning a spare-time income. The examples that follow cover only the more popular fields, but that does not mean that there are not openings for those whose interests are more esoteric and rarified. A skilful restorer of damaged books, an expert on Edwardian tinplate toys, a collector of antique carpentry tools will all find ways of turning their skill or knowledge to good account. What is more, in the process of acquiring that skill or knowledge they will probably have gained a pretty good idea of how much it is worth and to whom.

This whole area is one where careful market research is extremely important before you start out; not just to establish that there is a market and that you have the means of reaching it, but also to discover how much competition you are going to face. Goods which might find a ready market in an area which attracts tourists and has the gift shops and boutiques that go with them, may be a hopeless prospect in an industrial centre; there may be a need for a saddler or a watch repairer locally, but if that need is being met by an efficient and established service then it will be hard to break into the market, unless you can offer great improvements on their quality or price.

There are City and Guilds certificates in most of the fields covered and, even if you are already skilled it will probably be worth your while to take one at some point. Many courses—evening classes and others—are available in most areas and The National Institute of Adult Continuing Education (19B de Montfort Street, Leicester) publishes a guide to residential courses; West Dean College, Chichester specialises in art and craft subjects and one of their short residential courses might be a good means of refining your skills. There are also several organisations concerned with fostering craft work, running galleries and courses and awarding grants or prizes. They include: The Crafts Council (12 Waterloo Place, London SW1Y 4AU), regional Arts Associations (a list of individual associations and local craft guilds is available from the Crafts Council), The Wales Craft Council (20 Severn Street, Welshpool, Powys SY21 7AD), and The Crafts Section of the Scottish Development Agency (Rosebery House, Haymarket Terrace, Edinburgh EH1 5EZ).

The Women's Institutes (National Federation of Women's Institutes, 39 Eccleston Street, London SW1W 9NT) are also active in the field, running courses at their college and providing outlets through their market stalls.

Art and design

The borderline between the amateur and the professional, the full-time and the spare-time artist, is infinitely flexible: essentially, a full-time artist is one who achieves sufficient success or has a large enough private income to cease being spare-time. This entry does not deal with commercial type art and design which is covered in Chapter 6; it is likely that anyone seeking a spare-time income from those sources will have either a job or some formal qualifications in the field already. But, what about the Sunday painter who yearns to see a red sticker on his picture and a cheque in his hand?

The crucial factor is, of course, whether anyone will want to buy your work. You must be quite clear that if the income is more important to you than the enjoyment, you may have to compromise with your own personal tastes: Alexander Calder or Andy Warhol may have collected thousands of pounds for a piece of striped canvas or a blown up comic illustration in a Madison Avenue gallery, but, alas, the chances are that the tastes of your potential customers run more to sunsets, horses, and breaking waves.

The obvious starting point in the search for buyers will be your local art society; most hold regular exhibitions and even if they can't sell all your pictures they will give you an idea of what does, and doesn't, sell and the kind of prices your fellow artists get. If you have a local gallery then by all means approach them, but if not then hotels, restaurants and other local establishments may be willing to display and sell your work in exchange for a commission. Market stalls are another possible outlet, especially if you have a market within reach which already has an established array of arts and crafts stalls.

If you specialise in, for example, portrait work or natural history subjects, it may be possible to look farther afield. For example, several artists have successfully sold simple portraits by mail, getting a photograph as reference and producing a line or pastel work for a fixed fee. Publishers are always on the lookout for book illustrators, and if you have a largish collection of work it may be worth a trip to London to show it around to art directors of firms which specialise in this field.

Unless you hit the big time, you will probably not aspire to a London exhibition, and the commissions charged by London dealers (as high as 50 per cent) can be a major disincentive to do so; but it may be worth submitting your work to the Mall Gallery which regularly mounts exhibitions on behalf of a number of groups, and which does not demand any sort of exclusive arrangements with the artists who exhibit. If, on the other hand, you start to get regular work in book or magazine illustration you should probably consider getting an agent to look after your affairs—terms and fees vary widely and a good agent will be well worth his commission even though rates go as high as 25 per cent. The *Writers' and Artists' Yearbook* (A & C Black) lists established artists' agents.

Hourly earnings: Impossible to say.

Car: Not necessary.

Time and commitment: Variable.

Start-up costs: Relatively small.

Further information: Working for Yourself in the Arts and Crafts, 2nd edition (Kogan Page).

Bee-keeping

This is not a venture to embark upon unless you already have considerable experience, or are prepared to spend time and trouble gaining it. But there is a ready market for British honey in many places, if only as a change from the imported and blended varieties that fill most supermarket shelves; and if you can arrange matters so that your bees concentrate their efforts on heather or clover, so much the better. Honeycombs are also very popular indeed, and virtually unobtainable outside specialist, and usually very expensive, shops; but combs are perishable as separated honey is not, so the supply if not the demand will be seasonable. Also, bees that have to make their own natural wax produce less honey than those provided with ready-made combs.

If you live in the country and have a large garden, then, provided local farmers have not turned the landscape into a prairie of barley or oilseed rape (which makes unsatisfactory honey) there is no reason for not siting your hives in your own backyard. But even if your immediate neighbourhood is unpromising, you need not despair: many farmers will allow you to keep hives on their property, often in exchange for no more than a few pots of honey, and fruit farmers will positively welcome you. You will, of course, be expected to take care of the hives and to situate them where the bees will not get in the way of the farm's business—or vice versa.

As bee-keepers will be well aware, quite a major investment will be needed if you are going to keep bees on a substantial scale. Though it may be possible to acquire hives and other equipment second-hand, this will take time and involve attending local sales and auctions. The other equipment, frames with wax filling, separating machines, etc are all costly items, let alone the bees themselves.

The easiest market to reach is probably local grocers, farm shops and market stalls, but teashops and hotels may be a possibility in some areas and, if you are producing special honeys (clover, heather, etc) it is also possible to sell to quality food shops outside your immediate locality, or even to sell by mail order. There are clubs or societies in some areas and it may be possible to join, or initiate some collaborative sales effort with your fellow members, run stalls and exhibitions at local events and so forth.

Unless you have space for all your hives nearby, a car or light van will be essential for transporting hives, collecting swarms, and for your regular visits to tend your bees and collect the honey. Some space will also be required for storage, separation, packing, etc. A small shed or garage will suffice.

Hourly earnings: Impossible to quantify on an hourly basis, but from a single colony of bees it should be possible to earn £30 per annum.

Car: Likely to be essential.

Time and commitment: Though bee-keeping takes a lot of time, much of the work can be organised to fit in with other commitments. Long term, however, the commitment must be a strong one.

Start-up costs: It is best to start gradually, buying more equipment as and when you need it. However, a single colony of bees will cost around £50, and you could easily spend £350-£400 on basic equipment—more if your plans are ambitious.

Breeding or boarding animals

Whether this is even a remote possibility will obviously depend in the first instance on where you live. For the town or suburban dweller it is almost certainly a non-starter. But if you live in the country, have an extensive garden and no very near neighbours then it becomes a realistic proposition, provided you can devote yourself to it full time. Animals, like children, need care and attention throughout the day.

Though dogs and cats are the obvious choices, it is worth pointing out that people make substantial incomes from breeding and selling many other creatures—ornamental waterfowl, the various ornamental strains of chickens and bantams, even tropical fish. But in all these fields, building up a reputation, and getting to know the ropes and the personalities involved will take a matter of years rather than months. Whatever you are breeding, you will certainly have to get involved in showing, for in the case of virtually every kind of creature your best credentials will be a case full of rosettes, at least from county or area competitions if not on a national level. Of course, a single bitch with good pedigree producing a litter of pups a year can bring in a useful sum of money, but if your aim is a regular spare-time income you are going to have to be more ambitious.

You are also likely to find yourself involved in fairly substantial starting-up costs. Remember that you not only have to house your stock properly for their sake, but most of your sales will probably involve customers visiting your premises to inspect or collect their purchases. Ramshackle buildings, bad conditions and a seedy atmosphere will cost you sales. Food is also going to be a substantial item—in the case of dogs at least, a slaughterhouse in the district may be able to supply offal and other waste which will be cheaper and no less nutritious, though probably less pleasant for you to handle than all those cans advertised on TV.

Unless your property already qualifies as 'agricultural', you will probably have to apply for planning permission for any new building required, and you may also find yourself due for inspection by your local Environmental Health Department and, possibly, the animal welfare societies. (In the case of dogs, if you keep more than two bitches for breeding purposes you will *have* to register with the Environmental Health Department.) If you are running your enterprise properly and efficiently, you, of course, have nothing to hide or fear from such visitors. A good source of advice at the outset is your local vet. Apart from the fact that you will certainly be relying on his services a good deal, he will be able to advise on housing and equipment, feeding, etc and may also know of potential competitors, partners or sources of help and advice. Whatever creatures you get involved with, there will be a club or society at national level, running shows and competitions, and providing a link between breeders and fanciers. There are also many magazines covering the species or breeds.

Providing boarding accommodation for cats or dogs may be an attractive alternative to breeding, or a venture to be run in conjunction with breeding, if you cannot afford the time it may take to build up a reputation as a breeder. On the other hand, boarding is likely to be a very seasonable business—you may be turning customers away in July and August, but many months of the year can be all too quiet. You will also require planning permission and substantial insurance coverage against loss or damage to other people's pets. You may consider that hideous mongrel a worthless beast when compared with your priceless pedigree Pomeranians, but the owner may argue that its sentimental worth to him, his children or his mother-in-law entitles him to considerable damages if the Alsatian in the next kennel eats it for a midday snack, and the courts may support him too.

If you go in for breeding on a serious scale, you will almost certainly be concentrating on pedigree breeds, and looking to a market beyond your immediate locality. If you do not already have the beginnings of a breeding stock, then the purchase of animals and/or stud fees could be a major item of expenditure. If you plan to make a worthwhile income it is no use buying anything but the best; purchasers will study the ancestry of puppies, for example, with the same concentration and for as many generations as the House of Lords assessing a dubious claimant to a peerage. They will not be impressed by claims like the hand-painted notice that stands outside a minute bungalow on the south coast offering: 'Pedigree Puppies — All Breeds'. What you can charge varies enormously, depending on the breed and its current popularity, the quality of your breeding stock and their show records and your own standing in the breed society and the dog or cat (or goldfish, guinea-pig or rabbit) world in general. Most pedigree dogs or cats are sold through classified advertisements in the appropriate magazines which, in the case of gun dogs and other working breeds, include the sporting and country journals like *The Field* or *The Shooting Times*.

You can quickly establish the sort of rates which local boarding kennels or catteries are charging by calling and enquiring, asking your vet or checking advertisements in the press. The current averages run from £20 to £30 per week, depending of course on the breed, its size and appetite for food and exercise. If you are out at work all day, there will have to be someone at home capable of taking responsibility for your charges.

If you are really experienced with dogs then another possibility, or a further diversification, may be training. There is a steady demand, for instance, for gun dog trainers. But this is not something to go into unless you have a lot of experience and credentials, in the form of prizes from field trials, to back you up. You will need kennels in which to keep your pupils and a good deal of wide open space, or access to it, in which to train them.

The whole field of animal or bird breeding and/or boarding is one in which it is all too easy to underestimate overheads. The start-up costs, as we have established, are likely to be heavy, but so are food bills, the vet's account, transport of your charges and travel for yourself — a successful couple of days at a major show can involve a good many drinks and meals for contacts, customers and judges as well as nourishment for the Supreme Champion.

Hourly earnings: Impossible to estimate for breeders, but you will certainly have to reckon on an initial period when a lot will be going out and very little coming in.

Car: Almost certainly essential.

Time and commitment: Very substantial. Keeping, exercising and feeding even a small breeding stock of many creatures can involve hours of work every day, and once you have embarked on the venture you are committed every day for years ahead.

Start-up costs: This will depend on what kinds of birds or animals you have in mind, but in many cases they will be measured in hundreds, if not thousands, of pounds.

Further information: Running Your Own Boarding Kennels (Kogan Page).

Carpentry and cabinet-making

For the committed handyman and woodworker, this is a strong possibility. It is also a field in which it is perfectly possible for the beginner, who has time to spare, to learn the trade. Many technical colleges and evening institutes run courses on carpentry and cabinet-making, some on a part-time basis, others as short residential courses for those who already have the basic skills.

You will of course need a reasonably sized workshop and a substantial tool-kit. It is not possible on a regular basis to do quality work on the kitchen table after dinner; you need one room at least in which your bench can be set up permanently, your tools to hand and work in progress safe from accidental damage. Good woodworking tools—and it is certainly a false economy in this field to go for anything but the best—are now very expensive indeed, so unless you already have the nucleus of a good kit, you are going to have to reckon on an initial investment of four or five hundred pounds for the bare minimum.

The good news is that a very big demand for your services almost certainly exists. The gap between the man who can knock up a cupboard or a shelf provided it involves only standard softwood mouldings and wire nails and the craftsman who can restore a Sheraton table, at a price, is a large one and mostly unfilled by full-time professionals. If you are equipped and competent enough to repair good but not enormously valuable (that is a job for the real expert) furniture, if you can make things like refectory tables or kitchen units to order, etc you should find your services much in demand.

Local advertising, word of mouth recommendation and, perhaps, a helpful antique shop which will recommend you to customers is probably all the promotion you will need. A car or van is likely to be essential for collecting and delivering, transporting materials, etc.

A fair hourly rate for you to charge for your time would be £6-£8, plus your overhead costs and materials. If a job requires the purchase of special timber, say seasoned oak for a refectory table, then you should ask the customer for a payment on account to cover the costs.

Hourly earnings: £6-£8.

Car: Almost essential.

Time and commitment: Good work cannot be hurried, and you are unlikely to find this worthwhile unless you have at least eight hours a week to spare, but the commitment can be tailored to suit your own needs and the amount of work you take on.

Start-up costs: Could be considerable if you do not already own tools and equipment.

Making fishing tackle and fly-tying

As the angling market has expanded over the past 20 years, many large businesses, such as the Swedish ABU, have succeeded in gaining the lion's share of the tackle market. But there are still many small, specialist suppliers, both shops and mail order businesses, and manufacturers, some of whom regularly subcontract work to part-time home workers or may be willing to stock and sell your goods.

The two most obvious areas are the finishing of rods, probably using fibre-glass, carbon or cane 'blanks' supplied by the manufacturer, and fly-tying. No one has yet found a way of mechanising either satisfactorily, and the input of labour and skill is high compared to the cost of materials. A visit to a large tackle shop, or a study of the many angling magazines, will quickly yield a list of names and addresses to contact. It may be a difficult business to break into if your angling ambitions never got beyond the worm-and-bent-pin stage, but if you are a fisherman you will probably have an idea of possible starting points and contacts.

Fly-tying is a business carried on almost entirely by

home-workers. It demands patience and dexterity, but a minimum of equipment—the basic tools can be purchased for well under £50. You will also need a stock of materials—silk thread, hooks and various arcane materials such as seal fur, peacock herl, feathers, etc—which can be obtained from specialist suppliers. You will also need to read the angling press regularly—many fly-fishermen have a passion for the new and experimental and firmly believe that trout feed on a 'flavour of the month' system, rejecting the fly that worked last year in favour of more up-to-date designs.

You can seek work from one or more of the big tackle manufacturers, in which case you will be essentially a subcontractor, but if you live in an area where there are local fishing waters—and now that many reservoirs are stocked with trout, this means most places—you can also find outlets for your flies yourself. Local tackle shops are an obvious possibility, but many clubhouses or fishing lodges carry a stock of flies as well.

If you are a fisherman, it will certainly help to spread the word about your wares if you contribute to the angling press. From the customer's point of view there is a lot of difference between the anonymous artificial mayfly nymph that his tackle shop happens to stock and a mayfly nymph personally made by 'old so-and-so who is always writing' in his favourite magazine. You will have to reckon with the fact that sales, if not production, of flies is limited to the months from April to October.

Hourly earnings: £3-£4.

Car: Not essential.

Time and commitment: This is work that cannot be hurried, but it can be fitted in easily around other commitments and does not demand a week-in, week-out routine.

Start-up costs: Minimal, and if you already make some of your own tackle or flies probably zero.

China repair

Not work for the slapdash or butter-fingered. Before taking on the repair of other people's valuables, you will certainly want to take a professionally taught course (see pages 155-6) even if you have already learnt a good deal by reading and trial and error.

It will be hard to get enough business locally without some

contacts, such as antique shops or dealers, who provide fairly regular work. It is also possible to operate through the mail, in which case you should not only insure your parcels with the Post Office but also investigate a policy covering goods in transit with your insurers.

The equipment needed is relatively small and cheap, but you will obviously need a workshop with good light and free from disturbance. One of the most important points is to know the limits of your own abilities and competence; do not undertake work on rare and valuable objects unless you are absolutely confident of doing a first class job—your skill, or lack of it, could affect the value of a piece by hundreds, if not thousands of pounds.

Hourly earnings: Aim at £6-£8.

Car: Not essential.

Time and commitment: This is slow, painstaking work which cannot be rushed; moreover, like all repair work, it involves a willingness to undertake jobs at short notice if you want to build up a clientele and keep their goodwill.

Start-up costs: Perhaps £300-£400.

Metalwork and jewellery

There is an enormous spectrum of craft work open to those who have skills in working with metals and/or minerals. The materials range from the relatively cheap, such as copper or brass and stones which can be purchased in any craftshop, to gold, silver and gem- or semi-precious stones. Unless you have the resources and the talent to serve the very top end of the market, producing objects of real distinction and using the more valuable materials, in which case private commissions become a possibility, you will be well-advised to make sure that you can find outlets for your work before launching into it on a business footing. Much will depend upon your skill, obviously, but unless you have local shops willing to stock your goods, or contacts with more distant outlets, you may find that you have to devote a disproportionate amount of time to actually selling, rather than making them.

Craft, souvenir and art shops are obvious possibilities, and market stalls can offer another worthwhile outlet. But you can also try to persuade hotels, for example, to exhibit a showcase of your work, or even tackle local jewellers or department stores—you will certainly stand a better chance if the materials you use are of local origin, or if you can, in some other way, find a peg on which to hang your sales pitch.

The stocks you require and their cost, the space and equipment needed for the work and the level of skill required will, clearly, vary enormously. In general, of course, the more valuable the material and the more work involved in handling it, the higher the price it will command. Thus the silversmith may have a fairly low rate of production but get a good price for each item, whereas someone who makes jewellery out of more commonplace materials will have to aim at a much higher rate of production to achieve the same income. It will pay to specialise in a relatively narrow range of goods, enabling you both to speed up production and simplify selling. Because, once out of your hands, your produce is anonymous and probably relatively small in size, you may well find it worthwhile to contrive some form of packaging which gives you an opportunity both to print your name and address as the maker and also draw attention to the item in a display. If you work in gold or silver you will, of course, have to send each item to one of the Assay Offices for assay and hallmarking.

Hourly earnings: Anything from £3 for those producing simple, inexpensive work to £10 and upwards for those whose work, in precious materials, approaches professional standards of competence and artistry.

Car: Not essential in most cases.

Time and commitment: Will vary according to product; in some cases the sales, at least, may be strictly seasonal.

Start-up costs: Anything from a few pounds to a thousand pounds or more if you lay in stocks of precious metals or need elaborate tools.

Model making

There is a market for models—architects often need them for clients or competitions, shops for display, and the manufacturing industry for exhibitions or promotions—but the competition is very stiff indeed. A quick tour of the Model Railway or

Model Engineers' Exhibition will reveal that there are dozens of model makers of almost incredible patience and skill, so this is no field to venture into unless you are really pretty good at it— an ability to lend a hand with the kids' Airfix kits is not the same thing.

To gain a name you will certainly need to join the appropriate societies and take part in exhibitions, etc. After that it will be a matter of contacts and recommendation, but museums, display and exhibition contractors, architects and major stores are all potential customers worth a direct approach—work may not be instantly forthcoming but at least you will be on their books when the need arises. Film and TV production companies also have a need for model makers, but many of them employ professional staff or have established contacts with workers in the field.

Hourly earnings: Around £6-£8.

Car: Not vital.

Time and commitment: Almost infinite, if you share the perfectionist instinct of most model makers.

Start-up costs: You probably won't be considering the field unless you already have an established workshop.

Photography

While it may be possible to earn a little cash by acting as 'official' photographer at weddings and other events, doing portrait sittings and generally competing with the high street photography shop, it will prove a hard way to earn a steady additional income. The availability of sophisticated equipment at affordable prices, the extent to which it now supplements the photographer's skills and the fact that most families number at least one keen amateur photographer among their ranks mean that the services of a 'professional' are less likely to be needed than in the past.

Much the best long-term method for making money from your camera is to concentrate on a particular range of subjects and gradually develop outlets for your pictures. There is a steady demand, for example, for bird and natural history photography, for scenic or architectural pictures from various regions of Britain or, if you travel, of foreign countries, etc. Whatever field you concentrate on, you will easily be able to discover the magazines and publishers who have a requirement for pictures. When you become established, you may get commissions from them, but at the start you will undoubtedly have to shoot a good deal of film 'on spec'. You can also put your work in the hands of an agent; many specialise in particular subject areas and a list can be found in *The Writers' and Artists' Yearbook* (A & C Black).

Local camera clubs can be a useful introduction to fellow enthusiasts and, via their exhibitions, an outlet for your work. As with paintings, local galleries and public libraries may also be willing to mount exhibitions, though you should probably look upon participation in these as a means of widening your reputation rather than as an immediate source of income.

Magazine and book publishers' fees will depend upon the use being made of the picture (how large is the reproduction? is it colour or black and white? is it being used on the cover? etc); the circulation of the magazine or the size of the first printing of a book, and the markets in which it will be sold will also affect your fee (if a book is to be published in the USA as well as in Britain and the Commonwealth, for example, there will be a much more substantial fee).

It is going to take time—years rather than months—to make a name for yourself and develop the market for your pictures, so you cannot look to your camera as the source of a quick or urgently needed buck; but if you have the resources, the skill and, of course, the talent you can join the relatively small number of spare-time photographers who make a worthwhile income from their hobby.

Hourly earnings: Impossible to quantify; much will depend not only on your success but also on the subjects you concentrate on.

Car: Again, whether or not this is important will depend upon the kind of work you undertake.

Time and commitment: In most cases you will have to reckon on your photography absorbing much of your available spare time, and long-term commitment will almost certainly be a 'must'.

Start-up costs: These will be considerable in terms of time and film expended.

Pottery

If you already practise the craft for pleasure, you will know that it requires a good deal of space—doing it for profit will probably mean you need more. You may also, especially if you hope to produce in volume, need bigger equipment—pug mill, kiln, etc.

Pottery is a very competitive field, there are many professionals as well as amateurs of near professional standard, so you will do well to assure yourself that there really is a market for your line before you invest time and money. As well as craft and souvenir shops, galleries, hotels, teashops, etc may offer outlets in the right area. Much will depend upon where you live and how much competition is already established.

Initially it may be possible to make use of a kiln at the local school or college if you do not already have one, and if there are other potters in the district there is quite a lot of scope for sharing facilities as well as for bulk buying.

Simply on its commercial merits, pottery cannot be rated very highly as a source of spare-time income. You will be competing in a crowded market and, in many cases, with mass produced goods. However, most people who go into the work will probably do so for the very good reason that it offers much pleasure and satisfaction and/or because they are confident that they have the skill and talent to break through and establish a name for themselves. At that point, of course, the financial picture will change too; a potter whose work is in demand can expect to earn a handsome income from it.

Hourly earnings: £3 might be a reasonable target initially.

Car: Not essential, though useful for carrying supplies, delivering goods, etc.

Time and commitment: Potting is time-consuming and cannot be done satisfactorily in short bursts. The work can, however, be reasonably easily fitted in around other commitments.

Start-up costs: If you do not already have adequate equipment these could be a major item.

Spinning and weaving

Natural wool has been making something of a comeback over recent years, at the upper end of the market at least, and in many areas there is a ready sale for homespun wool and hand-woven materials.

If you are prepared to face up to the amount of labour involved in preparing a fleece by hand you can buy your raw material direct from farmers, otherwise the Wool Marketing Board will advise you where to obtain supplies. If you limit yourself to spinning, your obvious outlets are woolshops and, if your output justifies it, the occasional small advertisement in an appropriate magazine.

Weaving, of course, will involve obtaining a loom—quite an expensive acquisition, even second-hand. However, whether you weave wool which you have spun yourself or buy in materials, weaving offers scope for creativity in design, and the product, in the form of finished cloth, commands a good price. You will obviously have a head start if you live in an area with a tradition of weaving or of producing cloth of a particular kind. How you sell it will depend upon where you are and what you produce. You may, for example, be able to build up a private clientele for tweed, sold in lengths for dressmaking; or you may find a drapery shop or store willing to promote your goods. Mail order and small advertisements are other possibilities. Clearly, if you have a partner, or can organise a co-operative effort with fellow craftsmen, you may be able to mount more ambitious marketing schemes than would be the case with your own produce alone.

However, a loom is not the sort of thing which fits comfortably into the average front room, nor will the rest of the family want to live with the constant click of shuttles, so weaving is not something to undertake unless you have a largish space that can be used more or less permanently.

Hourly earnings: £3-£4 would be a reasonable target.

Car: Not essential.

Time and commitment: Spinning and weaving is slow, painstaking work and you will not produce a worthwhile output unless you can spend a good deal of time on it.

Start-up costs: Could run to several hundred pounds if you have to buy a loom.

Watch and clock repair

The decline of the high street watchmaker, a victim of electronics and quartz crystals, has created good openings for the spare-time worker, but you will need qualifications. The British Horological Institute (Upton Hall, Upton, Newark, Nottinghamshire NG23 5TE) offers correspondence courses and some colleges or evening institutes provide classes.

Though you need relatively little space and no vastly expensive equipment, you do need a room that remains undisturbed and can be exclusively devoted to the work. It must also have good light. A stock of spare parts and bits and pieces can be built up from stalls and jumble sales, but the main input will be your time.

Local advertising or, in some cases, advertising in a largish regional paper, is probably the best means of finding work; but you can approach local jewellers—if they have given up repair work (as so many have) they may welcome someone they can pass enquirers on to. If you are sufficiently qualified and experienced to cope with antique clocks, then shops and dealers are another obvious source and you may also consider advertising in magazines such as *Country Life*.

Hourly earnings: Varies from area to area. The British Horological Institute advise enquirers to check rates for skilled engineering workers (eg toolmakers) in their local area, and base their charges on a comparable rate.

Car: Not essential.

Time and commitment: Both substantial.

Start-up costs: Modest.

Toymaking

Unless you are making soft toys (dealt with under 'Other sewing work', page 152), you will probably do best to concentrate on fairly elaborate and expensive goods, first, because this is the one field where you do not face competition from mass produced toys—where indeed, the unique, craftsmanlike nature of your product is part of its attraction—and second, because you are faced with selling not hundreds of cheap items but a few expensive ones. Dolls' houses and furniture, rocking horses, etc are likely to be the things to go for. If you live in a wealthy neighbourhood, it may be possible to get private commissions for such things, otherwise your outlets are obviously the sort of shops which cater to the wealthy—and their kids. One thing at least is going for you; if you produce something really desirable for one child, all his or her friends are going to be pestering their parents for something similar. If you think that the exquisite doll's house you spent hours working on is going to be wasted on that little barbarian Esmeralda Ffolkes-Blueblood, look at it this way: she will be a much better advertising medium than anything you could afford.

Small advertisements in, for example, the rather posh county magazines that now flourish in many areas might work; or what about getting the local department store to use one of your products as a centrepiece for their Christmas display? Mail order is also a possibility using, say, a coupon in one of the upper-crust women's magazines. You will need a reasonably sized workshop or room and, probably, quite a lot of tools and equipment. Do take particular care to ensure that the paints and other materials you use are safe and non-toxic.

Hourly earnings: Aim at £5-£6.

Car: Not essential, though probably very useful.

Time and commitment: Both likely to be substantial.

Start-up costs: Low, provided you already have tools and equipment; if not they could run into several hundred pounds.

Picture framing

This is a craft in which the complete novice who is prepared to invest time in gaining knowledge and experience can hope to reach a high enough standard to make it a source of income. There are, however, two drawbacks. First, because of the enormous range of materials, styles and taste—professionals may work with anything from gilded plaster to burnished steel—you will have to carry quite a lot of stock, unless, that is, you are willing to accept the waste of time and money involved in buying materials separately for each job. Second, you will probably need to find a regular source of work other than private customers. Picture framing is, for most people, something they have a need for only rarely, and the bills for most jobs will not be vast.

You should, therefore, aim to establish contact with antique shops, local galleries, art and photographic societies and other sources of a regular flow of work.

You will need quite a lot of space—not only for your tools and workbench, but also for stock. A car is also pretty important for collecting and delivering work, visiting potential customers, etc. You will have to invest time and money in producing a range of samples from which customers can choose materials and styles—it is unlikely that you will want to venture into the more elaborate techniques and materials, but even simple wooden frames come in a bewildering variety of shapes and sizes.

Hourly earnings: £5-£6 is a reasonable target for labour costs; remember to add on the cost of materials.

Car: Lack of one will be a major handicap.

Time and commitment: The work is time-consuming, and if you are to build up a regular clientele among shops or galleries, as suggested, you will have to be prepared to take on work at short notice and do it rapidly.

Start-up costs: You could spend several thousand pounds on tools and presses, but it is probably best to start with the basics, then pick up second-hand items as you go along. You need a good mitre box, a stapling gun, glass cutter and two large tables as working surfaces.

Upholstery

If you have the necessary skills, or can spare the time to acquire them at one of the many evening or short residential courses available, upholstery is a very promising source of spare-time income. Professional workers are increasingly few and far between and very expensive. It is, however, a relatively long-term venture—the work is time-consuming and you must reach a high standard of workmanship before putting your services on the market.

It is certainly not something to be undertaken unless you have a good deal of space available or if you live cheek by jowl with your neighbours—upholstery involves a good deal of hammering! It will also simplify your life, and that of your customers, if you have a large station wagon or small van—with the best will in the world a three-piece suite cannot be crammed into the average family saloon.

Normally your customers will purchase their own fabrics, but they will look to you for advice on how much is required and the suitability of materials. Your stock will not, therefore, need to be heavy. You will normally have to provide estimates before starting a job and you should allow for the unforeseen problems which old furniture can reveal when stripped of its coverings.

Local advertising and word-of-mouth recommendations should be sufficient for finding work, though local antique shops and even junk shops may be willing to put in a good word for you. A variation on the theme, if there is a hiatus in the flow of customers, is to comb the second-hand furniture markets for items which you could refurbish 'on spec' and then resell. But beware of filling your workshop from floor to ceiling with decaying furniture that looked like a bargain at the time—one or two carefully chosen pieces, where restoration will produce a really valuable item, will prove more rewarding than a dozen 1940s settees which were cheap and nasty even when new.

Hourly earnings: You can probably aim at paying yourself around £5 an hour.

Car: Vital, indeed something larger will be greatly preferable.

Time and commitment: Considerable: the work is labour intensive and you will need to put in several hours a week on a regular basis.

Start-up costs: Provided you have work space available these need not be high.

Saddlery and leatherwork

Curiously, as the English countryside has been overrun with children's ponies in the great riding boom, the local saddler has continued to be a fast-vanishing species. (The same applies, incidentally, to blacksmiths, but that is probably beyond the scope of the spare-time worker.) This means that though many horse or pony enthusiasts have no difficulty in buying new saddlery, they do face a problem when it comes to repairs and the purchase of special items.

Helpfully, for the spare-time saddler, the horse-riding community tends to organise itself into groups—pony clubs, riding schools, hunts—which are easy to find and reach; if, therefore, you can get a foothold in one of these camps you should be able to build up a reputation fairly quickly.

Not all leatherwork, of course, is concerned with horses and petshops; camping or outdoor shops and department stores may have room for your goods. There is also repair and restoration work to be had from antique shops, etc.

Depending on your line of work, you may need to carry fairly heavy stocks and you may also need some specialised equipment and a sizeable work space.

Hourly earnings: You should aim at £4.

Car: Probably not essential.

Time and commitment: Good leatherwork takes much time and patience; you will need to give several hours a week to the work and, especially if you undertake repairs, you will have to be prepared to accept jobs at short notice.

Start-up costs: Unlikely to be heavy.

11. A Way With Words

Over 50,000 books are published in Britain each year and goodness knows how many million words appear each week in papers, magazines and journals. The vast majority of the raw material for this output comes from spare-time authors. Moreover, all those words which pour from the printing presses need editing, proofreading and, in some cases, indexing and translating: all fields where the spare-time freelance may be even commoner than the full-time professional.

Speaking very broadly, spare-time writers fall into two groups: those whose primary talent is for writing as such and who find, in their imagination or their surroundings and experience, things to write about; and those who have or acquire specialised knowledge for which other people are prepared to pay.

If your talent is simply for writing itself, you will have to build up a reputation, and at the outset at least, no one is going to pay you a penny until you have done the work. If, on the other hand, you have expertise on a particular subject—it may be your profession, your hobby or some part of your experience—then you may be in a position to seek a commission to write on that subject even if you have no particular talent for the business of writing itself.

All the opportunities described in this chapter require a place to work in peace and quiet, free from interruption or distraction. You cannot tackle any form of writing or other work with words unless you are free to give all your attention to it, and you will probably need space to spread yourself as well. So a study, or a room in the house where you can shut yourself away, scatter papers without inhibition and not be responsible for checking that the vegetables haven't boiled dry or that the kids are doing their homework, is essential. There are rare and admirable

individuals who can isolate themselves from their surroundings, however chaotic, but unless you are one of them you are
going to have to declare a 'no-go zone' for the rest of the family
around your place of work. You are also going to have to set
aside time on a regular basis; unless you want to find yourself
starting the same paragraph five times or spending half an hour
trying to reconstruct a chain of thought, you simply cannot pick
up this sort of work and drop it again at a moment's notice in
favour of something else. With the possible exception of editorial work, all the jobs require a typewriter and at least rudiment-
ary typing skills; no publisher or editor will be prepared to
consider a submission in manuscript or to receive a translation
that is not neatly typed, and even an index requires to be typed
out when it is complete. You can, of course, employ a typist but
this will eat into your profits considerably.

Writing fiction

'Everyone', it is said, 'has a novel in them.' To which the publisher's reader, contemplating a pile of manuscripts, is often
tempted to reply: 'And 99 per cent of them should not be
allowed out.' The first thing to make clear if you are thinking of
writing a novel for the first time is that you are undertaking a
gamble which is going to involve a great deal of work and in
which the odds are stacked against you very heavily indeed. If
you are a real novelist this will not, of course, deter you in the
least: what you write may be good, bad or indifferent, but it will
be something you write because you want to write it. You
should, however, be aware that, especially in recent years, the
vast majority of 'literary' or 'quality' fiction has proved
unrewarding for author and publisher alike. The rising cost of
book production, coupled with the effect of cuts in public spending on sales to libraries, has made work by even well-established
novelists a dubious proposition for publishers. So, even if you
find a publisher, do not expect miracles; you may be doing well if
your income from a novel exceeds £1000.

If you are looking for a more substantial and reliable income
from novel writing, then you should turn your mind to the 'commercial' or 'category' book. The adjectives are not derogatory,
and there is no reason why a 'commercial' novel should not be a
very good novel or the 'category' novel excellent of its kind;
what they do demand, however, is that the author writes to

please as wide a readership as possible as well as to please himself.

The commercial novel is something in constant flux—if man-eating monsters were the rage two years ago, then they may well have been replaced by wrecked supertankers, financial catastrophe or whatever. There is no reason, if you are invent-ive, why you should not start a new craze. The category novel, however, is relatively clearly defined as a 'thriller', 'science fiction', 'romance', etc. 'Westerns' are in decline at present. The advantage of the classifications is that they fall into an estab-lished niche in the publisher's catalogue, the paperback rack or the public library; people like to read them not because they are different but because they are variations on a set theme. This is not to dismiss the skill, ingenuity and the quite genuine feeling and subtlety that can go into their writing—indeed will have to if they are to be successful. What it does mean, however, is that the newcomer has clear standards against which to measure his work.

The chances of your first novel—whatever its nature—being accepted will be much improved if you have an impeccably typed manuscript, and if you offer it to the right publisher in the right way. *The Writers' and Artists' Yearbook* (A & C Black) gives the names and addresses of British publishers and an indi-cation of the fields in which they are active. *The Writers' Hand-book* (Macmillan) is another useful guide. But an even better guide to the firms that are most likely to be interested in your novel can be gained from an hour or two browsing in a bookshop or public library looking at recent novels comparable—or so you hope—with your own.

Remember that the only way the publisher can judge your work is by reading it. No useful purpose, beyond wasting your own time and his, is served by asking if he is interested in a novel about a plot to 'poison Warrington' or 'to blackmail the Home Secretary's aunt'; and even less by calling personally to explain what the book is about. Provided that you have done your homework and the firm concerned does publish your sort of book, the best thing you can do is to send off the manuscript (do make sure you have a copy, neither the Post Office nor pub-lishers are infallible) with a straightforward letter and a cheque or postal order to cover return postage.

An alternative to submitting your work directly to a pub-lisher is to employ a literary agent. In return for a commission, usually 10 per cent of the earnings, an agent will submit your manuscript, negotiate terms and generally look after your interests. You must, however, be prepared for the fact that agents, like publishers, have to be discriminating. They cannot become involved in submitting every book that comes across their threshold to every possible publisher. The advantages of working through an agent (*The Writers' and Artists' Yearbook* gives names and addresses) are that most publishers will give more careful consideration to a manuscript that carries the endorsement of a reputable agency, and if your book is accepted an agent will be in a position to make sure that you get a fair deal. On the other hand, many publishers, and some authors, feel that an agent can be an unhelpful, even malign, intermediary. It also has to be borne in mind that there are bad agents, just as there are bad publishers; the publishers you can judge by their wares in the bookshop and library, the agents are more difficult for the newcomer to evaluate.

Whether you are dealing with a publisher direct or through an agent, their offer for publication will take the form of an advance, that is, a minimum guaranteed sum of money (normally paid half when you sign an agreement and half on publication), a scale of royalties and a proposal as to how income from the sale of rights should be divided. The advance in the case of a first novel by an unknown author may be very small, perhaps no more than £500 or £750, but remember it is not what the publisher hopes you will earn but the minimum he feels reasonably sure of. Established authors and those who have reason to be confident of their book's success will naturally press for as high an advance as possible, not only for the sake of the income, but also because the payment of a large advance represents a commitment on the publisher's part to put all his weight behind the book.

A royalty scale for a novel will usually start, if it is to be published in hardback, at 10 per cent of the published price and rise, after several thousand copies have been sold, to 12½ per cent and then 15 per cent. On copies sold overseas the scale will either be lower and based on published price, or similar but related to the publisher's net receipts, ie the published price less the discount given to booksellers. Paperback royalties normally start at 7½ per cent for home sales and 6 per cent for export sales and rise to 10 per cent or 12½ per cent and 8 per cent or 10 per cent respectively. As well as acquiring the right to publish

179

your book, the publisher will be granted certain rights in it. He will normally expect to have the right to license other editions (paperback editions, book club editions) in Britain and the Commonwealth, to give permission for reproduction of passages in anthologies, etc. He may also want the right to license American or translated editions, though if you have an agent he will probably suggest that he handles these aspects. The proportions in which income from sales of rights are divided can be crucial—the sums involved may be very much greater than the royalties you earn from the publisher's own sales. Generally speaking, the author's share goes from as little as 50 per cent up to as much as 90 per cent; it all depends on the book, the circumstances and the bargaining strengths of the parties.

The one thing you should never agree to, whatever the temptation, is to accept an outright fee from a publisher or to sell the copyright in your work—normal publishing agreements license the publisher to exploit the copyright, but it always remains your property and the publisher's licence ends if he stops making use of it. The novel that sold a few hundred copies and has been forgotten long ago may suddenly become a valuable property when you become successful, you never know!

Fiction is not only published between the covers of a book. A better market, at least to start with, may be offered by magazines or broadcasting media. Fiction these days is pretty much restricted to 'women's' magazines and, if your interests run in that direction, the 'girlie' and soft porn ones. This does not mean that only women or sex maniacs have a chance in the market. But it does mean that there is less scope for the straight adventure story, involving heroic tussles with giant anacondas or fearsome 'natives', than there was in the days of the 'boys' magazine. Unless they are serialising books or buying big names to promote their circulation, in which case terms will be negotiated on an individual basis, most magazines pay a standard 'wordage' rate for their fiction, usually calculated at so much per thousand words—the actual figure will vary widely with the circulation of the magazine. The same rules apply as when submitting a book to publishers: send your offerings, clearly typed, to the fiction editor and enclose return postage. *The Writers' and Artists' Yearbook* gives details of magazines regularly publishing fiction.

You will gain little as a beginner by employing an agent to sell your work to magazines, but if you are successful and can, perhaps, aim higher than the standard rates and contribute to several different papers or find a market for your work overseas, then an agent may become a near-necessity.

Breaking into the market for television scripts is a very tough prospect indeed, unless you already have an established reputation in an allied field such as novels, short-story writing or the theatre. A more likely *entrée* to the airwaves is via the radio. BBC Radio 4, in particular, still broadcasts a great deal of fiction, in the form of plays and short stories. You should submit the work directly to the producer of the programme you think most appropriate, or to the drama department at Broadcasting House, Langham Place, London W1A 1AA. The BBC publishes a guide, *Writing for the BBC*, which outlines the possible openings for freelance work over the Corporation's whole spectrum of activity.

The Society of Authors, 84 Draycott Gardens, London SW10 9SB and the Writer's Guild of Great Britain, 430 Edgware Road, London W2 1EH will both advise members on contracts, legal aspects, etc.

Hourly earnings: Impossible to quantify, they could be anything from zero to the moon.

Car: Not necessary.

Time and commitment: You have no obligation to anyone except yourself, but most experienced writers find that they work best on a regular daily schedule.

Start-up costs: Zero.

Writing non-fiction

Many non-fiction books find their way to publishers in exactly the same way as novels, as a completed manuscript, and if you have no obvious experience or qualifications which fit you to write a book on a given subject, then this is probably the course you will have to follow. But in some cases publishers will be willing to commission non-fiction works: that is, to sign a contract and pay the first instalment of an advance before you begin work. With an established writer, or someone whose reputation in another field makes him or her a desirable author, this is likely to be the publisher's usual method of buying non-fiction. It is less likely with the unknown tyro, unless you have some

181

knowledge or expertise that particularly qualifies you to write on a given subject. If, for example, you are a metallurgist or have devoted years to the study of Japanese lacquered cabinets, then you may find it relatively easy to find a publisher who will commission you to write about metal fatigue or the Japanese decorative arts, but they will not be interested in your projected book on economic policy.

In non-fiction, even more than with fiction, the right publisher is the key. Publishing houses specialise, partly because their lists reflect the interests and knowledge of their staff and partly because their marketing efforts are more effective if they have whole ranges of books on particular topics. If you are an expert in a particular field, you will almost certainly know which firms are active in your area; if you have any doubt, a look around a good library or bookshop where the stock is classified by subjects will help. Do concentrate on relatively new books — Bellweather & Co who published all the best books on ballet in the 1920s may have changed hands three or four times in the interim and may now be concentrating on concrete technology. For advice on contracts, agents, etc see previous entry on fiction. Except for the possibility that it takes the form of a commission to write a book rather than an agreement for a book already written, the contract for a non-fiction work is broadly similar to that for a novel. Do remember, though, that you may well be expected to find and pay for illustrations, negotiate the use of passages quoted from other people's works, and be responsible for the compilation of an index.

Non-fiction writing for newspapers and large, general magazines does not offer many opportunities to the spare-time freelance. Such media have full-time journalists on their staff, and usually accept freelance contributions only from established, professional writers or from 'big names'. They may require specialist contributors or outside consultants in particular fields, but this is work that is more likely to come when they seek you out as a result of a reputation gained in the field concerned than as a result of an approach from you. Smaller or more specialised magazines are a very different matter. In the case of those devoted to a particular business, profession, trade or interest, they may operate with a minimum of full-time staff and rely almost entirely on outside contributors to fill their columns.

Most successful magazines of this kind are constantly on the look-out for new writers and will welcome material of the right kind. What is essential from their point of view is that you have something new, interesting, exciting or controversial to say. You can obviously judge what sort of material they are interested in from the magazines themselves, but do not forget that what they really want is likely to be, not more of the same, but something just that bit different. Above all, beware of straying into the territory of one of their regular contributors who is likely to have quite an influence on what the magazine publishes on his pet subject and who will probably not welcome competition. The editor may welcome controversy on the 'letters' page, but he probably won't want to publish your article discrediting his most revered contribu or.

The great thing about journalism of this kind is that one piece of work will lead to another; a series of articles in one magazine may lead to an approach from a rival editor, an invitation to review books or address interested societies, or an enquiry from a publisher. Moreover, regular appearances in the press can bolster your professional reputation or become an asset in another spare-time enterprise. Once you have become established, and if your subject area is one that demands illustration, it may well be advantageous to ally yourself with a photographer who can illustrate your articles.

Most magazines pay for non-fiction contributions on a wordage basis, and the rates will depend on the circulation and cover price of the paper in question. You must be prepared for the fact that it takes time to build a reputation and become known and this is certainly not a field where success is predictable and income reliable—too much depends upon your skill in conveying information and making it entertaining.

Hourly earnings: Impossible to estimate where books are concerned. For journalism, after taking the time required by research into account, £8-£10 might be a fair target.

Car: Only necessary if a lot of research, and thus travelling, is involved.

Time and commitment: As with fiction, this is a matter of self-discipline.

Start-up costs: Zero.

Further Information: Writing for a Living, How to Write Articles for Profit and PR (Kogan Page).

Copy-editing and proofreading

Very few books go directly from the author's typewriter to the
typesetter. They are, to a greater or lesser extent, edited by the
publisher's own staff or by freelance editors. So the good news is
that there is a mass of work available; the bad news is that it is a
very overcrowded field and therefore it is often hard for the outsider to break into.

The degree of editorial attention which a manuscript needs
can vary enormously. In some cases it is simply a question of
checking that style and usage are consistent and conform with
the publisher's 'house style' in matters such as when to use capital letters, hyphens or punctuation; at the other end of the scale
are manuscripts which require drastic surgery or even a complete rewrite. Publishers obviously prefer to entrust major jobs
to people whose work they know and trust: a careless, slapdash
or over-hasty piece of work can cost hundreds of pounds in
printers' corrections and can sour relations between author and
publisher or badly harm the eventual sales of the book. Both
copy-editing and proofreading require a methodical mind, a
capacity for taking infinite pains in checking and rechecking
and a good working knowledge of English grammar and usage
as well as a 'feel' for writing. In the case of books on scientific or
specialised subjects, a background in a particular field of knowledge may also be essential.

The editor's Bible will be *Hart's Rules for Compositors*
(Oxford University Press) and most publishers will also supply
a house style sheet giving details of their firm's particular
whims or vagaries. If you go into either editing or proofreading,
you must familiarise yourself with the standard printer's marks
used in marking up copy; the British Printing Industries Federation, 11 Bedford Row, London WC1R 4DX will supply copies
of these. Experience in publishing, journalism, printing or
advertising work is a great advantage, if only in reassuring publishers that you are likely to know what you are doing. You will
require a good dictionary, probably some works of reference,
especially if you intend to specialise in technical or scientific
subjects, and access to a good reference library—in many cases
it is necessary to check the spelling of names, the accuracy of
titles and dates, etc.

Given publishers' natural inclination to give the first offer of
work to people they know and trust, the problem of getting

started boils down to getting yourself known and establishing a sound record of work. Within a publisher's office, the decision to do a particular job 'in house' or subcontract it to a freelance is likely to be taken by the individual editor or the managing editor (titles vary from firm to firm in a bewildering fashion). *The Writers' and Artists' Yearbook* gives names and addresses of British publishers together with their fields of activity. Unless you have personal contacts within the publishing business, which will offer you an invaluable head start, then the only course is to write to individual publishers, stressing, where applicable, your knowledge of subject areas in which they publish. Make no mistake, this is a hard field in which to get a start, but once you have established contacts and gained a reputation you can be confident of a regular supply of work. Copy-editors and proofreaders charge an hourly rate for their time, £6-£8 currently being normal, and invoice the publisher on completion. It is worth noting that not all publishers are as punctilious about paying bills promptly as they should be, and if you find yourself working regularly for one company it can be worthwhile establishing good relations with someone in their accounts department.

The one thing which will earn you thanks and loyalty from publishers is reliability. Book production schedules are prepared months in advance, and a delay at copy-editing or proofreading stage can throw them completely out of gear, so do not take on more work than you can handle, give a realistic estimate of the date by which you will be able to complete a job, and stick to it.

Hourly earnings: £6-£8 (more for difficult or rush jobs).

Car: Not usually necessary.

Time and commitment: Very variable. To edit a manuscript can take anything from a couple of days to six months, so your commitment will depend upon the amount and kind of work which you take on, but it will be difficult to secure regular work if you choose to do only an occasional job, and do not keep in touch with your customers.

Start-up costs: Zero.

Indexing

Indexing work is not recommended to those who lack an orderly mind and a capacity for taking pains. A good index is a minor work of art, but it is also the product of clear thought and meticulous care. As with editorial work, peace, quiet and concentration are essential.

Indexes are nearly always commissioned by publishers so the sources of work and the contacts to be cultivated are as in the previous entry, and the establishment of a steady relationship with one or more firms is equally valuable. Specialist knowledge is an advantage: few indexers could truthfully claim to be able to index all subjects ranging from advanced polymer chemistry to the history of art, and most indexers confine their indexing expertise to no more than four to six subject areas. Speed, promptness and accuracy are essential, for the index can only be compiled when the book has reached page proofs, the final stage before printing.

The Society of Indexers (16 Green Road, Birchington, Kent CT7 9JZ), while not formally a professional or qualifying body, has a panel of registered indexers and provides a full correspondence training course and it is certainly worth joining if you are taking up the work seriously. It publishes a half-yearly journal, *The Indexer*, and a quarterly newsletter, as well as holding regular meetings and conferences. It is active in maintaining standards and looking after the interests of indexers. It sends a list of members annually to UK publishers.

Indexers usually calculate their fees on an hourly basis, £8 being a basic hourly figure, but much depends upon the type of work required. A simple index of names only would take up less time than for example one on comparative social policy where entries for themes as well as people may be necessary and many of the entries will be analytical, that is, broken down into subentries and cross-referenced. To produce such an index you have to understand the author's argument thoroughly in order to interpret it in summary form.

Hourly earnings: Basic minimum £8.

Car: Not necessary.

Time and commitment: This will depend upon the amount of work you take on, but once committed to a job you may be expected to complete it quickly, and indexing can be very time-consuming. Your commitments are therefore likely to be substantial, at least for periods of several days at a time.

Start-up costs: Zero, but a computer is becoming increasingly useful and for some publishers, necessary.

Translating

The British, being an insular race, appear to have a minimal interest in translated literature, and the number of novels or works of general non-fiction which are published in English translation has been steadily declining for several years. As a result, competition for this kind of translation work is intense and standards are very high. An experienced translator of straightforward prose will expect to be paid a fee of about £30 per thousand words of English translation, rather more if the original language is a difficult or obscure one. Translation work is normally commissioned by the British publisher, so there is no point in approaching foreign authors or publishers with offers of your services, and to translate a book 'on spec' is almost certain to be a waste of time and effort.

Scientific, technical and commercial translation is a much more promising field. In the case of scientific or technical work, the demand from publishers of books and journals is substantial, but you do need qualifications in the subject matter as well as the language. Again, the people to approach are the British book or periodical publishers, and you will obviously do well to choose a company which specialises in the field where your own scientific qualifications lie. Rates will vary from £30 to £40 per thousand words upwards, with languages such as Chinese and Japanese, where qualified translators are few and far between, commanding a considerable premium.

Businesses also sometimes need translators, though since they will often need the work done at very short notice this could be a more difficult area for spare-time work. Most firms with a regular requirement for translators use one of the agencies active in the field and unless you are in a position to make your own contacts with local businesses you will certainly find an agency essential. Rates vary widely (and you will have to allow for the agency's commission) according to the complexity of the material and the original language. Japanese, Chinese and, in this instance, Arabic have a rarity value.

You will obviously require a comprehensive and up-to-date dictionary, or dictionaries if you work in more than one language, and, if you are planning to do scientific or technical work, you may need a fairly substantial range of reference books which could be costly.

The Translators' Association, a subdivision of the Society of Authors, 84 Draycott Gardens, London SW10 9SB, can advise on fees and other contractual matters and, among other things, awards annual prizes for distinguished work in the field. The Institute of Translation and Interpreting (318a Finchley Road, London NW3 5HT) is a professional body for technical, scientific and commercial translators; it provides careers and training advice, and runs regular workshops. Careers information is also available from the Institute of Linguists (24a Highbury Grove, London N5 2EA); the Institute administers a qualifying examination for professional translators, the *Diploma in Translation*.

Hourly earnings: Depend greatly on your rate of work; they could average out at anything between £7 and £20 an hour.

Car: Not necessary except in special cases.

Time and commitment: Like writers, translators find that they work best with a regular discipline, and a couple of hours each day is probably a minimum.

Start-up costs: Zero to £200-£300 if you have to purchase reference books.

12. Buying and Selling

The first necessity for selling is, to put it bluntly, that you must be likeable. People will buy things they don't need or want if they like the person doing the selling; equally, they may resist buying urgent necessities from people they dislike. But charm is not enough; you also have to know a lot about what you are selling, you have to be willing to take pains and suffer fools gladly, you must have the ability to think fast and, above all, you have to enjoy the work. All these points apply even more forcefully to spare-time selling. For if you are selling something in your spare time, the chances are that the person who is buying it is doing so in his spare time as well, and he will not be grateful to you for interrupting it if he likes neither the goods nor your company.

Dealing

It is possible, of course, to deal in almost anything under the sun, from copper futures to cornflour; but in the case of the spare-time worker, the choice is likely to narrow down in practice to one of the 'collectables'—antiques or works of art or craft. It is a tempting field, if only because it offers a chance to combine business with pleasure and appeals to the gambler in us all—maybe, just maybe, you will chance upon a Rembrandt in the flea market.

The best advice on the subject is probably that if you can afford to lose some money then, in the long term, you may make some; but if you are looking for a surefire way of earning some extra income then don't rely on dealing. Certainly it is not something to be embarked upon if your need is urgent or your cash resources slender. In order to sell successfully you need stock, which means investing in purchases, and time; the forced sale will usually be a disadvantageous one. Moreover, you will certainly be well-advised to start out by doing some odd dealing just for the fun of it, without having to worry too much about whether you win or lose.

If you do decide to have a go then you should probably choose a limited field and specialise in it. You are matching your knowledge and wits against experts with a lifetime's experience in the business and it makes sense to shorten the odds by concentrating your efforts on a narrow front—you can't hope to master the whole range of expertise involved in something like porcelain, but you may hope to hold your own at least in a small area of it. You will need a good deal of spare time; your buying will probably have to be done at small sales up and down the country, and your selling either from a stall in one of the major markets or privately to shops or collectors. Neither process can be rushed. A car is going to be essential and so is a fair amount of cash; to sell you are first going to have to buy.

One specialist line that may be worth some thought, if you have a sound basis of knowledge and experience, is the second-hand book business. It is possible to sell either through the small, second-hand bookfairs which are now a regular feature in many places, or, if you have the time and patience to build up a mailing list, by compiling and sending out regular catalogues. Even within this field, specialisation—on, say, nineteenth century science or first editions of modern poets—will be the most profitable course to adopt.

It is impossible in the space available to go into any detail about the world of dealing, but it is worth emphasising that this is almost certainly not the business for you unless you already know far more about your chosen subject than could possibly be covered here.

Hourly earnings: Impossible to say—but this is one field where they may quite possibly be a minus rather than a plus.

Car: Probably an absolute necessity.

Time and commitment: To earn any worthwhile and regular income you are going to have to work long hours much of the time.

Start-up costs: An initial stock in most fields is probably going to involve the investment of sums well into four figures.

Being a mail order agent

Mail order is very big business indeed, and largely the province of very big companies, but it relies upon the services of tens of thousands of very small businesses—the agents who actually sell the goods, with the help of the mail order companies' lavish catalogues, collect the money and deal with customers' queries and complaints.

In theory, being an agent is easy money. You contact the mail order firm and, provided they accept you and that you are over 18, there is nothing to stop you launching into business right away. The idea is that your customers select the goods they want from the catalogue supplied at regular intervals by the company (in most cases the range covers household equipment, clothes, toys and games, radio, TV, cheap jewellery, etc), you fill in an order form and send it back to the company, who supply the goods. Payment is usually made on easy terms, with regular weekly or monthly payments which you collect and send to the company after deducting your commission, which is normally 10 or 12½ per cent. As a bonus, you are of course entitled to purchase goods for your own use at the discounted price (ie less commission).

The snags are less evident. Not all mail order companies are as efficient as they might be and many agents have a whole repertoire of horror stories involving defective or wrongly delivered goods, payments that went astray and other accounting confusions and, of course, the problem of bad debts. You may be the most popular person on the street when you first have the glossy catalogue full of desirable goods at what look like bargain prices; but you may not be so popular six months later when you have to dun your neighbours for overdue payments, make excuses for the company's errors, and deal with people who want to return or exchange their purchases.

Also, a quick calculation will show that to make the effort worthwhile you are going to have to sell a lot of goods. To make a minimal two or three pounds an hour you have to sell something like £25-£30 worth of goods, and you collect the commission only as, when and if your customers make their payments. Given that the people you stand the best chance of selling to are friends, relations and neighbours, pause a moment and think how long it might take Aunt Agatha to make up her mind about a new winter coat, or how much nagging it took to get back the £5 you rashly lent to the lady across the road last month.

In short, becoming a mail order agent may be attractive for the chance it offers to acquire goods on advantageous terms, and it may produce a small income by way of commissions on other sales, but as a source of regular and substantial spare-time earning it is probably not a good bet for most people.

Hourly earnings: You will do well to clear £2 an hour.

Car: Not needed.

Time and commitment: You will have to invest a lot of time to gain a worthwhile return, though admittedly much of this may be spent in socialising rather than 'working' in any real sense. The commitment need not be long-term but, when it comes to collecting and accounting for payments, it can become a tiresomely drawn-out affair.

Start-up costs: Nil.

Party plan selling

If you become an agent for a party plan selling organisation your basic role is to organise parties—either in the evenings or at 'coffee time' around mid-morning—which you will attend and at which you will demonstrate the goods you sell and, with the help of the hostess whose house and friends you have borrowed for the occasion, take orders from the guests. Clearly, it is not a job for the socially unsure or the easily embarrassed. Unlike mail order, party plan selling is done on a cash basis, the money usually being collected from the customer at the party and the goods then delivered COD to the agent or the hostess. In most cases, therefore, it avoids the bad debt or slow payer problems of mail order. On the other hand, it is a harder 'sell'; instead of just providing a catalogue, the agent is expected to be capable of demonstrating the goods (some elementary training may be offered by the supplier) and to actively persuade the party-goers to dig into their pockets or handbags. Commissions are usually of the order of 25 per cent, and some firms offer incentive schemes to encourage their agents into an activist approach.

The field has in the past been something of a happy hunting ground for the get-rich-quick brigade, and you should avoid any firm that requires its agents to purchase more than a token demonstration kit. You should also discover how many other agents are selling the same products in your district—it may be very nice for the sales manager to know that three agents are, unbeknownst to each other, fighting it out for the market in a single district, but it will not be very remunerative for the agents. You should also make sure that you have seen and approve of the goods you are going to sell; you are unlikely to be successful if you feel half-hearted or worse about your wares. Study the small print of any contract you are asked to sign with great care and, if in any doubt at all, consult a lawyer.

You are almost certainly going to need a car—it is unlikely you will generate a business on a worthwhile scale unless you spread your net fairly wide. A good deal of time and energy will also be required, as setting up parties can be a complicated and wearisome job, calling for persistence and a lot of careful planning; moreover, many of the firms in the business do press agents to keep up a fairly constant level of activity, so you should be prepared to set aside quite a lot of time.

Hourly earnings: £3-£4 would be a good target, remembering that for every hour you spend actually selling you are going to have to spend several more in planning and preparation.

Car: Usually essential.

Time and commitment: Both substantial.

Start-up costs: Minimal.

13. No Ideas? Jobs Almost Anyone Can Do

This final chapter covers the opportunities of last resort, spare-time work which demands little skill and can be found at short notice. The drawback in most cases will be that the rates of pay are low and the work hard and often uninteresting. In other words, these are jobs you should consider only if your need is urgent and none of the other opportunities described appeal to you or fit your circumstances. One advantage is, of course, that the work can usually be dropped as rapidly as it is taken up, so once the need is abated you can look around for something more interesting. Many of the jobs described here are part-time employment from the tax and National Insurance point of view.

Cleaning

Most of us reckon that keeping our own homes spick and span gives us more than enough cleaning work to satisfy the Mrs Mop (or Mr Mop) in our make-up; but, done properly, the work is not unfulfilling. The rewards will not be high, £2-£3.50 an hour is usual, although you may be able to claim your travel costs on top of this. Contract cleaning—of fabrics, and carpets in private houses, or offices and supermarkets—can be better paid. Fortunately, for all types of cleaning, demand generally exceeds supply.

The first thing to decide is whether you want domestic or office work. Cleaning other people's homes has the advantage—or it may be a drawback—of personal contact with the customer and it is usually daytime work. Office cleaning is likely to be a more impersonal job and will certainly be done in the evening. In the case of domestic work a classified advertisement, or a card in a shop window in a likely looking area will probably produce as much work as you can handle— but do check the 'help wanted' advertisements first, you may need to look no further. Small local businesses, with premises that can be tackled by a single person, can be approached directly or through classified advertisements; again a glance at the local paper may reveal the firm that is already looking for you. Institutions such as homes for the elderly, hostels, etc usually have a need of cleaning staff as well.

You can look to your employers to provide the equipment and materials you need; don't become involved in carrying supplies around with you but make sure that all you need is kept 'in stock' at each place of work. You should beware of employers who expect you to double up as a babysitter or childminder, or ask you to undertake tasks like cleaning the first floor windows with a rickety step-ladder; you are not being paid to take care of the kids or to risk life and limb. Obviously, if and when you get to know your customers well, there will be occasions when a good deal of give and take is in order, but do not let it be assumed that this is a part of your duties.

Hourly earnings: £2-£3.50 (depending largely on where you live). £5 an hour is possible in London.

Car: Probably not required.

Time and commitment: Clearly, if you are to earn more than a pittance you will be working long hours, but normally you will be engaged on the basis that a week's notice on either side is sufficient to end the arrangement.

Start-up costs: Nil.

Being a tea- or dinner-lady

For no particularly good reason, tea-men and school dinner-men scarcely seem to exist—here is a whole new field for males to break into. For the moment though, we will use the old terminology only because 'dinner person' sounds faintly absurd.

Many smaller offices have resisted the doubtful attraction of automatic tea and coffee machines and still employ part-timers to brew and serve mid-morning and afternoon tea or coffee. Such jobs are often advertised, but a canvass of local establishments should soon produce a job if all else fails. Be warned, if you are good-natured you will almost certainly be taken advantage of. Everyone from the managing director downwards may

195

fancy a quick cup of coffee when you're not around—mysteriously, though, they are seldom so keen on a quick wash-up of the crockery used. The going rates for the work are likely to be around the £2 mark, so it is not a goldmine; on the other hand, for a single or retired person, it can be a pleasant way of keeping in touch and will not involve heavy work.

Schools, whether they prepare lunches on the premises or import them from a central catering establishment, all need dinner-ladies whose job it is to serve lunch, do the washing-up and, with the help of the teacher on duty, preside over the gastronomic bedlam at 'dinner break'. The school secretary will normally know if the school has need of more dinner-ladies and will be able to put you in touch with the official who deals with 'hiring and firing' staff. (In future the employer may be a private firm, supplying school catering on a contract basis, but you can still ask the school secretary to put you in touch with the firm's personnel department.) Clearly, this work can only be done by those whose spare time fits in with hours, usually 10.00 or 11.00 am to 2.00 or 2.30 pm, and the pay scales are not dramatic—£2.50 an hour would be average for the country as a whole.

Hourly earnings: £2-£2.50.

Car: Not needed.

Time and commitment: You will be working set hours, probably up to about four a day, and you can usually give a week's notice if you decide to quit.

Start-up costs: Nil.

Distributing leaflets or promotional material

This work is probably best left to schoolchildren and students on vacation. It is relatively easy to come by; employment agencies often have such temporary jobs on their books or PR firms may take on staff directly, but the pay is low and the work sporadic and deeply uninteresting—who really wants to stand outside a tube station in pouring rain thrusting bits of paper into commuters' hands? Or push leaflets through letterboxes? If you do undertake such tasks you can expect to be paid 1p-3p per leaflet, but you may be employed on a day-to-day basis and much of the work won't fit into most people's spare time.

Hourly earnings: Probably not much more than £1.50-£2.

Car: Unnecessary.

Time and commitment: The hours can be long but the commitment is non-existent.

Start-up costs: Nil.

Market research interviewing

This is a job you will probably not want to consider if you are looking for a spare-time income on a temporary basis, but it does have the virtue of being moderately interesting and demanding some skill and involvement. The best way of finding work is to register with one or more of the major market research organisations (you don't have to limit yourself to local ones, though the major firms are based in London they will in most cases want to get a sampling of opinion right across the country). Some preliminary training may be required and some firms organise short courses for prospective interviewers.

Your job is to get consumer reaction either to an established product or, more probably, a new one; to help the manufacturer discover not only what the public thinks of his goods, or would think of them if he decides to launch the product, but also how well his advertising is working and how people perceive the goods. In other words, you are not just discovering whether John Smith has tried and enjoyed, say, 'Hotpot—the curry in a carton' but whether, even if he hasn't, he looks upon it as a luxury item featuring regularly on the menu at stately homes or whether he thinks of it as rubbish which he would give to the dog. To ascertain vital facts like this you will be equipped with a carefully prepared questionnaire, designed not to sway the interviewee but, provided you do your job properly, elicit his real opinion, or the nearest he gets to one.

Some market research is carried out simply by stopping people at random in the street, but if you are working in your spare time you are more likely to find work interviewing people in their homes in the evening or at weekends. Increasingly, telephone interviewing is used for consumer research. Obviously, it takes a certain degree of confidence, if not brashness, to tackle total strangers and press them for their views on freeze-dried curry, toothpaste or toilet soap, so if you are the sort of person who agonises before asking a passer-by for the time this is probably not a job for you.

Hourly earnings: Around £3-£5.

Car: In some cases this may be helpful, but it is unlikely to be a necessity.

Time and commitment: Interviewing, properly done, is time-consuming work and if you are to get on to the books of a reputable company, and stay there, you will probably have to work fairly steadily and regularly.

Start-up costs: Nil.

Waiting

Serving in cafés and restaurants is a time-honoured standby for the teenager and student, but it can also be a useful spare-time job. Establishments which need labour in the evenings are obviously ideal, so you are more likely to find what you want in a restaurant or pub than in cafés which, typically, do most of their business between 9.00 am and 5.00 pm. Do not on the other hand imagine that you are going to walk into the kind of job that involves wearing elegant evening dress and debating claret vintages with the customers—waiting is far from unskilled, and unless you have several years' experience you are unskilled labour. What you do and how you do it will vary greatly with the place in which you find work. In an expensive restaurant you may find yourself dressed in an apron, restricted to clearing away dirty dishes and speaking only when you are spoken to; in the neighbourhood Italian restaurant on the other hand, you may be expected to cope with a number of tables on your own, and a tropical sweatshirt and a tendency to burst spontaneously into grand opera may be expected of you.

The rates of pay can vary as widely as the duties and the demeanour expected of you. The range runs from £2 an hour up to £4 or more, with extra for evening and weekend work. In many places, too, the work may be seasonal—waiters are about as much in demand in seaside resorts in winter as grass skirts are in Antarctica.

You can find waiting jobs through your local employment office, classified advertisements in the paper or simply knocking on the door and enquiring. Normally, the terms of employment will be a week's notice of termination on either side.

Hourly earnings: £2-£6.

Car: Not necessary, unless you take a job some distance from home which involves working late hours—as many do.

Time and commitment: In most cases this will be a five or six nights a week job, and though you can in theory switch in and out of work at will, beware of getting a reputation for unreliability or not sticking in a job.

Start-up costs: Nil.

Being a local councillor

A final thought, not totally frivolous. Local councillors are now paid attendance allowances, varying from council to council within a statutory limit, as well as being able to recover legitimate expenses. So, while it would be ridiculous to suggest that you stand for office just for the money, this may, if you are interested in and committed to politics, be as remunerative and interesting a way of combining business with pleasure as any other.

Hourly earnings: Variable, but far from handsome.

Car: Not needed.

Time and commitment: You will find, if you do your job well, that for every hour in the council chamber for which you draw an attendance allowance, you spend several more in unpaid labour coping with constituents' and other problems.

Start-up costs: Nil in cash, though a great deal in time and energy.

Further Reading from Kogan Page

Business Rip-Offs and How to Avoid Them, Tony Attwood, 1987

Debt Collection Made Easy, Peter Buckland, 1987

Do Your Own Bookkeeping, Max Pullen, 1988

Going Freelance, 2nd edn, Godfrey Golzen, 1989

How to Deal With Your Bank Manager, Geoffrey Sales, 1988

How to Prepare a Business Plan, Edward Blackwell, 1989

Readymade Business Letters, Jim Dening, 1986

Running Your Own Boarding Kennels, Sheila Zabawa, 1985

Running Your Own Catering Business, Ursula Garner and Judy Ridgway, 1984

Running Your Own Mail Order Business, Malcolm Breckman, 1987

Running Your Own Smallholding, Richard and Pauline Bambrey, 1989

Running Your Own Typing Service, Doreen Huntley, 1987

Simple Cash Books for Small Businesses, 2nd edn, Paul D Ordidge, 1989

Start and Run a Profitable Consultancy Business, Douglas A Gray, 1989

The Stoy Hayward Business Tax Guide, annual, Mavis Seymour and Stephen Say, 1989

Successful Marketing for the Small Business, 2nd edn, Dave Patten, 1989

Working for Yourself in the Arts and Crafts, 2nd edn, Sarah Hosking, 1989

Writing for a Living, 2nd edn, Ian Linton, 1987

cu/ar

Fish's Outline of Psychiatry

for Students and Practitioners

Edited by

MAX HAMILTON
MD, FRCP, FRCPsych, FBPsS

Nuffield Professor of Psychiatry, University of Leeds
Honorary Consultant to General Infirmary at Leeds
St James's (University) Hospital, Leeds
Stanley Royd Hospital, Wakefield

with a Chapter by

ALAN WESTON
MB, FRCPsych.

Consultant Forensic Psychiatrist,
Stanley Royd Hospital, Wakefield

THIRD EDITION

BRISTOL: JOHN WRIGHT & SONS LTD. 1978

First Edition 1964
Second Edition 1968
Third Edition 1978
Reprinted 1980

CIP Data:
Fish, Frank
    Fish's outline of psychiatry for students and
    practitioners. – 3rd Ed.
    1. Psychiatry
    I. Hamilton, Max II. Outline of psychiatry
    for students and practitioners
    616.8'9   RC454

ISBN 0 7236 0381 2

Printed in Great Britain by offset lithography by
Billing & Sons Ltd, Guildford, London and Worcester